Poverty in an Affluent Society

INQUIRY INTO CRUCIAL AMERICAN PROBLEMS

Series Editor · JACK R. FRAENKEL

Poverty in an Affluent Society:

Personal Problem or National Disgrace?

DAVID A. DURFEE

Social Studies Chairman
Sleepy Hollow High School
The Tarrytowns, N.Y.

PRENTICE-HALL, INC.   ENGLEWOOD CLIFFS, N.J.

Titles in this series:

✓ CRIME AND CRIMINALS: What Should We Do About Them?
 Jack R. Fraenkel

PREJUDICE AND DISCRIMINATION: Can We Eliminate Them?
 Fred R. Holmes

THE DRUG SCENE: Help or Hang-up?
 Walter L. Way

POVERTY IN AN AFFLUENT SOCIETY: Personal Problem or National Disgrace?
 David A. Durfee

COUNTRY, CONSCIENCE, AND CONSCRIPTION: Can They Be Reconciled?
 Leo A. Bressler and Marion A. Bressler

VOICES OF DISSENT: Positive Good or Disruptive Evil?
 Frank Kane

CITIES IN CRISIS: Decay or Renewal?
 Rudie W. Tretten

TEEN-AGERS AND SEX: Revolution or Reaction?
 Jack L. Nelson

✓ PROPAGANDA, POLLS, AND PUBLIC OPINION: Are the People Manipulated?
 Malcolm G. Mitchell

✓ ALIENATION: Individual or Social Problem?
 Ronald V. Urick

EDUCATION AND OPPORTUNITY: For What and For Whom?
 Gordon M. Seely

FOREIGN POLICY: Intervention, Involvement, or Isolation?
 Alvin Wolf

Prentice-Hall International, Inc.,
 London
Prentice-Hall of Australia, Pty. Ltd.,
 Sydney
Prentice-Hall of Canada, Ltd.,
 Toronto
Prentice-Hall of India Private Ltd.,
 New Delhi
Prentice-Hall of Japan, Inc.,
 Tokyo

PREFACE

The series *INQUIRY INTO CRUCIAL AMERICAN PROB-LEMS* focuses upon a number of important contemporary social and political issues. Each book presents an in-depth study of a particular problem, selected because of its pressing intrusion into the minds and consciences of most Americans today. A major concern has been the desire to make the materials relevant to students. Every title in the series, therefore, has been selected because, in one way or another, it suggests a problem of concern to students today.

A number of divergent viewpoints, from a wide variety of different *kinds* of sources, encourage discussion and reflection and illustrate that the same problem may be viewed from many different vantage points. Of concern throughout is a desire to help students realize that honest men may legitimately differ in their views.

After a short chapter introducing the questions with which the book will deal, Chapter 2 presents a brief historical and contemporary background so that students will have more than just a superficial understanding of the problem under study. In the readings that follow, a conscientious effort has been made to avoid endorsing any one viewpoint as the "right" viewpoint, or to evaluate the arguments of particular individuals. No conclusions are drawn. Instead, a number of questions for discussion and reflection are posed at the end of each reading so that students can come to their own conclusions.

Great care has been taken to insure that the readings included in each book are just that—readable! We have searched particularly for articles that are of high interest, yet from which differing viewpoints may be legitimately inferred. Whenever possible, dialogues involving or descriptions showing actual people responding and reacting to problematic situations are presented. In sum, each book

- presents divergent, conflicting views on the problem under consideration;

- gives as many perspectives and dimensions on the problem as space permits;

- presents articles on a variety of reading levels, in order to appeal to students of many different ability levels;

- presents analytical as well as descriptive statements;

- deals with real people involved in situations of concern to them;

- includes questions which encourage discussion and thought of the various viewpoints expressed;

- includes activities to involve students to consider further the issues embedded in the problem.

CONTENTS

Introduction

John F. Kennedy went to West Virginia in 1960 seeking votes that would help to make him President of the United States. He found the votes that he was looking for. He also found poverty.

There were not just a few poor people living in the hills and mountains of West Virginia in 1960, there were thousands. John Kennedy (and many others) also found poor people in New York. They found people living in want in Mississippi. They looked in California and North Dakota and in all of the rest of the fifty states of the Union. In every state they found poverty.

The evidence that poverty was widespread increased. One victim of poverty in a Chicago slum area reported:

I would say that there must be 100 people in this neighborhood who go to one garbage can or the other for food regularly. I would say 100 at least. A lot of them are really dependent on that food. When they come to the end of their welfare check, and if they dig diligently, they can live it out.[1]

Another victim, a migrant farm worker, described conditions in a camp:

The hollow square where the truck stood was paved with dusty rubble. Three long wooden shacks, once, but not recently, whitewashed, bounded three sides of the square; the fourth side lay open to a beanfield. A patch of woods concealed the camp from the highway.

Each shack had a row of doors opening into the square. A

---

[1] Excerpted from Kenan Heise, *They Speak for Themselves*. Chicago, Ill.: The Young Christian Workers, 1965.

scrawly number painted in black identified each door. All the threes were painted backward, and on each six and each nine the circle appeared on the wrong side of the stem as though children had been practicing writing in a looking glass. The doorsills were a good foot from the ground and there were no steps. To serve instead, some had cement blocks laid in front of them; a few had makeshift ramps of boards; three or four had inverted washtubs; some had nothing at all. Beside every door there was a window. There were no screens. Here and there stood trash cans spilling over with rubbish waiting to be hauled away. None of the cans had lids, and it all looked and smelled like the accumulation of several days. . . .

The morning sun poured hotly down on a sprawling woodpile; on a clothesline hung with diapers and little girls' dresses; on a derelict washing machine; on four slender iron pipes, one in each corner of the square, each rising two feet high and each topped by a water faucet. In the middle of the square a rusty, old-fashioned iron cookstove rested on the ground against the wall of a shanty. The shanty had a stovepipe in the roof, advertising that there was at least one more stove inside. That wasn't all that was in there, either, because through the shanty's open door a voice out of a jukebox told the world, *I've got everything, I've got you.*[2]

Another resident of Chicago described the effect of being poor in a rich society, saying, "I'm nothing more than a dishwasher. I make $8 a night, six nights a week. My take home pay is around $42. I'm nothing. I'm like an ant. They can step on me anytime they want." [3]

The discovery of great numbers of poor people in America took many citizens by surprise. The country was, after all, the wealthiest that the world had ever known. It was a country of "affluence," one in which there seemed to be more than enough for all. As far as these citizens could see, there were already surpluses, and production was increasing every year. It was true that they occasionally encountered a poor person, but not millions of men, women, and children. There were a few hundred, perhaps, but not millions! Not even thousands! Millions of people living in poverty couldn't really exist. Wouldn't they have been seen?

Author Michael Harrington provided an explanation for this apparent contradiction.[4] He reported that failure to see the poor was due to

---

[2] Excerpted from Louisa R. Shotwell, *The Harvesters: The Story of the Migrant People.* Copyright © 1961 by Louisa R. Shotwell. Reprinted by permission of Doubleday & Company, Inc.

[3] Excerpted from Kenan Heise, *They Speak for Themselves.* Chicago, Ill.: The Young Christian Workers, 1965.

[4] In his book *The Other America: Poverty in the United States.* New York, N. Y.: The Macmillan Company, 1962.

the fact that, though numerous, they had become isolated and invisible. He described two Americas. The first was a familiar place. It was a land of plenty and comfort; a land flowing with goods and services; a land in which people did not ask themselves, "How can I ever manage to get the things that I need?" but rather, "What do I want next?" The "Other America" was different. It was a place of want and despair. It was a land of poverty!

The amazing thing about all of this is not that poverty existed but that its existence was such a shock to so many people; not that a problem *was* discovered but that it *had to be* discovered.

Poverty has become a popular topic since Mr. Kennedy made his trip and Mr. Harrington wrote his book. If nothing else, the riots which have struck dozens of American cities since that year, riots with their roots in destitution and discrimination, have caused Americans to become concerned.

In 1964, President Lyndon B. Johnson announced that the United States would undertake a "War on Poverty." Since that time new programs have been introduced at the national, state, and local levels. Some have been designed to improve the housing and diet of the poor and otherwise lessen the effects of poverty. Others have been intended to bring an end to poverty itself.

A storm of controversy has raged around these programs. All have been criticized—some for trying to do too much, some for trying to do too little, and some for attempting the wrong things. There is no general agreement as to how the war on poverty should be fought, who should fight it, or even whether it should be fought at all.

Part of the controversy that has surrounded the various programs stems from some fundamental disagreements over the nature and extent of poverty in the United States. Not everyone who set out to look for poor people in the 1960's found as many as Mr. Kennedy or Mr. Harrington. While all agreed that there were some poor Americans, all did not agree that there were anywhere near the 30 to 70 million claimed by the more pessimistic investigators. Critics of these high figures pointed out that they were based on the number of families reported by the 1960 census to have incomes below $3000 a year. Many people with incomes below this arbitrary poverty line lived a pretty good life, they argued.

Other dissenters raised serious questions about the severity of poverty in America. They pointed out that with very few (if any) exceptions, being poor in America was not the same as being poor in India or Haiti or drought-stricken Botswana. They argued that poverty in America was not absolute poverty, the kind in which people actually starved to death, but a relative kind of poverty. People had enough to live on; they just didn't have as much as others in the society. Poor people in America, they said, are frequently better off than people of average means in other countries on this globe. Presidential candidate Barry M. Goldwater noted in 1964 that: "As our production and income levels have moved up over a hundred years, our concepts of what is poor have moved up also —and they always will! It is like greyhounds chasing a mechanical hare. You can never catch up. There will always be a lowest one-third or one-fifth." [5]

Just how much poverty is there in the United States? Where are the poor people to be found? How serious a problem is it? Is it also a problem for the affluent in America? For the nation as a whole? Is it possible to estimate how much it would cost the country to eliminate poverty? Can we estimate the cost of not eliminating it? Unless we can answer such questions, any kind of intelligent action is impossible.

There are poor people in America whether they number in the tens of millions or only in the hundreds of thousands and whether their poverty involves absolute misery or merely relative discomfort. What causes poverty? The problem cannot be dealt with until we have at least some answers to this question. Taxpayers will not be willing to support programs designed to improve the lives of the poor unless they believe that they have a responsibility to do so. If antipoverty programs are to succeed they must attack the roots of the problem. Why are poor people poor? Is it due to laziness? To lack of intelligence? Could they stop being poor if they were only willing to make the effort? Are they perhaps merely people who were unlucky enough to be in the wrong place or possess the wrong skills at the wrong time? Are they casualties of the industrialization of the country? Or might they be the unintentional victims of measures which were designed to help them but which backfired? Could it be that they are poor because of discrimination practiced against them by other individuals or groups?

These are difficult questions to answer, but then, if the problem of poverty were a simple one, it would have been solved long ago.

In fighting a modern war those weapons that are most effective in defeating the enemy are also those that are most likely to have side-effects. Radioactive fallout can be dangerous to the nation that employs nuclear weapons. Though modern medicines can be amazingly effective in battling disease, they may also produce side-effects which can do more harm than the medicine does good. The same is true of weapons available for use against poverty. Government, for example, can obviously be a potent instrument in the struggle against want. Could there be side-effects of increased governmental power, however, which must be guarded against?

---

[5] From a speech given before the Economic Club of New York, quoted in *Vital Speeches,* Vol. 30, February 1, 1964.

Oscar Lewis [6] has insisted that there is a culture of poverty, that people living in poverty differ from those living in affluence not only in their behavior but in their basic values and attitudes. Can we be sure that the values and ways of the affluent majority are so much better than those of the poor? Would the destruction of the values and institutions peculiar to the poor necessarily make this a better society? Might not the poor be able to teach their economically more fortunate fellow citizens some important lessons? Can poverty be eliminated without making America a culturally and spiritually poorer nation? Are there any aspects of poverty which should be preserved? Once again, such questions are difficult to answer.

In fighting a war against poverty, just as in fighting a war against an enemy armed with guns and tanks, it is not enough just to react blindly whenever the enemy attacks. An intelligent plan of battle must first be developed. Preparation of such a plan requires a great amount of information and understanding. A number of questions designed to elicit this kind of information and understanding have been asked above. Among these are the following:

1. What do we mean by "poverty"? Is the problem of poverty in the United States today really serious enough to necessitate a "war"? If so, why was this problem not "discovered" until 1960?
2. Why are people poor? Is it anyone's fault?
3. How much poverty exists? Who are the poor?
4. What effects does poverty have on the people in the society who are not poor? On the society as a whole?
5. How can we deal with the problem of poverty? What kinds of solutions are available? What side-effects must be guarded against when attempting to alleviate poverty and eliminate its causes?

The chapters which follow should provide information that will help you come to your own conclusions about these questions.

---

[6] In his book *La Vida: A Puerto Rican Family in the Culture of Poverty—San Juan and New York*. New York, N. Y.: Random House, 1966.

Is There Anything New About Poverty?

2

"There is an ugly smell rising from the basement of the stately American Mansion." [1]

Poverty is certainly nothing new. Man has had to contend with it throughout his history. If the human race has somehow managed to survive thus far in spite of all this poverty, is there any special reason to be concerned about it now? If anything, there is less poverty today than there has been in the past. Is there something new about it now that makes it an urgent problem? Or is there something new about American society today that makes the presence of poverty more intolerable than it was in the past?

There is something new about American society today, for America has performed an economic miracle. With a population that exceeds 200,-000,000, this nation has managed to create factories and farms so productive that they are able to provide not only enough for all but plenty for all. The average American today is able to consume quantities and varieties of goods and services that were beyond the grasp of even the wealthy élite of previous centuries.

It is not necessary to go too far back in history (or too far from the shores of the United States) to learn of countries in which only a favored few could write their names or read the books that were available. In America today the young person who has not attended high school is looked upon with suspicion, and efforts are made to get every-

---

[1] Gunnar Myrdal, *Challenge to Affluence.* New York, N. Y.: Random House, 1963.

one into college. Instead of having difficulty finding materials to read, as was the case in the past, the average American finds that he cannot keep up with all that is thrust upon him.

Just a short while ago only the wealthy could afford professional entertainment at frequent intervals. Today's American of modest means has but to turn a dial to be able to choose from among several kinds of performances. He may complain that it isn't all morally elevating, but he cannot complain that it isn't available.

Just a short while ago only the prosperous could afford to own a means of transportation capable of moving along at a speed of ten or fifteen miles an hour. Today it is assumed that the average man will own at least one automobile. In addition, jet transportation is available whenever 70 miles an hour on the highway seems unbearably slow.

Many parents in times past found themselves hardpressed to provide complete sets of clothes, including shoes, for their children. More and more children today are embarrassed if they have to wear the same articles of apparel to school twice within the same week.

One shortage, it is true, still exists—that of housing. Even this shortage, however, is a sign of a society of plenty, for it comes not from a failure to build new homes but from an increase in family units. Grandparents, parents, and children used to share a house. Today each generation expects a place of its own.

In the past, men dreamed about cornucopias and talked about Gardens of Eden, but their real life was one of scarcity. Certainly there were periods in history in which there was plenty for some. Great powers, from the Assyrians and Babylonians of ancient times through the Incas of Peru to the colonial powers of the Nineteenth and Twentieth Centuries, tried to gain plenty for their own people by conquering and exploiting other lands. There was plenty for the rulers, but not for the ruled. Other peoples, such as the citizens of ancient Athens and the plantation owners of the Old South, managed to achieve plenty for themselves by using the labor of slaves or serfs. There was plenty for the masters, but not for the slaves.

Enough for some but not for all; this has been the story throughout history. People had accepted the Biblical idea, "For ye have the poor with you always. . . ." [2] And then, suddenly, in the middle of the Twentieth Century, it appeared that "always" had ended. A new way of life with plenty for all had begun—or so many thought. John Kenneth Galbraith provided a popular name for this way of life when he titled his book *The Affluent Society*. Poverty in America today is different from poverty in previous ages because it exists within the context of this affluent society.

---

[2] Mark 14:7.

The Growth of a Land of Plenty

Rich human and material resources, hard work, and opportunity created this affluent society.

Millions of immigrants came to America because they saw here an unlimited potential. One historian has suggested that this potential for plenty is the key to understanding American character and institutions.[3] Americans never felt it necessary to have the government own and divide all the wealth or to establish rigid social classes to determine how the wealth would be divided. Why? Because they believed that there would be enough goods and opportunities for all. In other countries an individual could have comfort and plenty only if he took from others and left them in want. America with its seemingly unlimited resources suggested the possibility of a society in which each individual could have all he needed without depriving anyone else of his rightful share. Slavery was, of course, an exception to this, one that can be most generously explained by saying that it existed because it was the potential and not the reality that was unlimited at that time.

Those who came to America found a land rich in resources. The fertile lands of the central and southern sections of the Atlantic coast made agriculture profitable during the colonial period. In many of the colonies this agricultural prosperity was based on the labor of indentured servants and slaves brought by force from Africa. The Atlantic Ocean fostered fishing and commerce in the New England colonies. Farming, fishing, and commerce provided a base on which American prosperity could be built, though they could not, by themselves, create a land of plenty for all.

In the early Nineteenth Century textile mills and other factories became more and more common in the United States. Production climbed rapidly, and a growing prosperity attracted immigrants by the hundreds of thousands to American shores. These immigrants contributed to the growth of America, building the railroads which spanned the continent and manning the factories which turned out ever-increasing quantities of goods. These immigrants, however, although they were often better off than they had been in their native lands, seldom enjoyed plenty. Although wages for unskilled workers were higher in America than in Europe and the Orient, prices were higher too. The steady flow of new workers into the country and obstacles which prevented the formation of strong unions made it difficult for workers to bargain for a larger share of the profits of production.

---

[3] David Potter, in his book *People of Plenty: Economic Abundance and the American Character*. Chicago, Ill.: Univ. of Chicago Press, 1954.

In the late Nineteenth and early Twentieth Centuries the increases in production were more dramatic than ever. The invention of mechanical harvesters and planters and the development of scientific farming methods made it possible for American farmers to produce more than the nation seemed able to consume. The formation of giant corporations and the development of mass production methods made it appear that production could outrun need. There was a financial panic in 1893, and the economy turned downward temporarily between 1900 and 1910, but these were just minor exceptions to the rule of steadily growing production and consumption.

Even the Great Depression of the 1930's did not shake this faith in America's ability to produce enough and to spare. True, the nature and severity of the Great Depression did lead some experts to believe that the United States' economy had become stagnant. They argued that all of the basic products that man needed for the good life had already been invented and produced and that from now on the country would have trouble finding people who could use the tremendous numbers of products that her farms and factories could turn out.

The Second World War helped to show that they were wrong, as it provided a temporary demand for all of the goods that could possibly be produced. American factories showed that they were able to turn out just about as many consumer goods as they had been able to while the country was at peace and, at the same time, enough weapons and ammunition to bring the largest scale war in human history to a successful conclusion. The productive capacity of America had, indeed, become amazing. Furthermore, technology was providing even more efficient ways of increasing production every day. There appeared to be nothing that the economy could not accomplish. The average standard of living in America had gone up and up, and the percentage of people who could be classed as poor had gone down and down. There were still a few people who lived in want, but it seemed as if it would be just a matter of time until they too would enjoy the full benefits of the affluent society, the society which produced such a torrential flow of goods that its chief problem was getting rid of all that it had rather than figuring out how more could be produced.

This is not to say that everyone in the middle of the Twentieth Century was satisfied. As production and consumption had increased, so had desire. Mr. Smith could not be satisfied unless he kept up with, or perhaps was able to get ahead of, the Joneses. But the Joneses had more now than they had ever had before. The symbol of the affluent society was not the man who had plenty and was satisfied. It was, rather, the man who had plenty and felt that it was only natural to expect to have more.

Poverty Becomes "Invisible"

Under these conditions, the typical resident of suburban America did not give much thought to the question of poverty. Certainly few high school and college students from middle-class backgrounds talked about or even considered the possibility of a career dedicated to the elimination of poverty. Critics of the young people of the 1950's, indeed, often accused them of being too eager to get jobs in "big business," jobs that would insure them steady employment until it was time to retire, a generous pension provision, and perhaps even a company-supplied burial plot upon death. Many seemed to feel that it was foolish to take economic risks to make gains for themselves, and unnecessary to sacrifice themselves by taking low-paying social service jobs to help others. The economy would provide plenty for all without risk or sacrifice.

Such an attitude was understandable. Conditions had just recently returned to normal following the Depression and World War II, and the poor had not yet become very vocal in their demands. Many Americans who were better off, in fact, could ignore poverty because they did not see it or hear of it. This had not been the case during the Great Depression. In the 1930's, poverty was everywhere. In the great cities there were men on street corners selling apples. In the parks, frequented at times by those fortunate enough to still have jobs, were "Hoovervilles" of tarpaper shacks thrown up by the unemployed. The suburban housewife, especially if her home was near a railroad or main highway, was frequently interrupted by knocks at the rear door which told her that another member of the army of unemployed, men forced to abandon their homes and families and wander about the country, was seeking odd jobs or a handout of food. In rural areas farms on which mortgages had been foreclosed or which had just been abandoned were common. Throughout the land newspapers and radio broadcasts emphasized the severity of the Depression and described the unemployment and poverty that it had brought in its wake. The government, under the New Deal, made deliberate efforts to bring information about the Depression to the people. Franklin D. Roosevelt, in his "Fireside Chats," tried to present the picture of the Depression as a common problem of all Americans. He called on all to join in a common effort to end it.

The Depression hit all towns and cities and millions of families. The unemployment rates during the 1930's shown on the following chart show how pervasive the problem was during that decade, especially when compared with the figures for the years before and since.

It wasn't easy to ignore poverty during those Depression years, but it was easy to ignore it in the 1950's. By the end of World War II poverty was no longer distributed evenly across the country. It had become

UNEMPLOYMENT IN THE UNITED STATES

Year	Average number of workers unemployed	% of the total civilian labor force
1900	1,420,000	5.0
1910	2,150,000	5.9
1920	1,670,000	4.0
1925	1,800,000	4.0
1930	4,340,000	8.7
1932	12,060,000	23.6
1934	11,340,000	21.7
1936	9,030,000	16.9
1938	10,390,000	19.0
1940	8,120,000	14.6
1945	1,040,000	1.9
1950	3,142,000	5.0
1955	2,654,000	4.0
1960	3,931,000	5.6
1965	3,456,000	4.6

concentrated in pockets which were frequently hidden away. The families of the comfortable had moved from the cities with their slum areas into the suburbs. True enough, the breadwinner who commuted into the city to work might encounter an occasional panhandler asking for a dime or quarter, but such panhandlers appeared more as evidences of human weakness than as symptoms of a wide-spread social problem. They could be dismissed as individuals lacking in strength of character who couldn't make their way in a society of opportunity and so had turned to alcohol instead.

Even the trip into the city on the railroad, a trip which usually took the commuter through the older and poorer sections of the city, began in the 1950's to be abandoned by the great majority of commuters. Free-ways, parkways, and thruways, on which he alternately raced and crawled, took the commuter from suburb to office without the need or opportunity for a glance at the poor or their homes. His wife, in the meantime, had given up shopping trips into the city in favor of more convenient excursions to a suburban shopping center. Television even made it unnecessary for those desiring a wide choice of entertainment to travel into the city to find it.

Just about every community had its block of poorer homes tucked in behind the downtown stores or along the railroad tracks, but they were out of the way. Poverty, it appeared, was less of a problem than was crabgrass in the suburbs.

Rural poverty could also be ignored. Americans who wanted to get back to nature and see the farms could travel to the large areas of fine farm land where giant farms, often corporately owned, showed prosperity. To reach vacation lands, it was no longer necessary to follow slow roads through poor hill country areas or regions where men farmed sandy marginal soil. The same superhighways that took men into the cities took families to the mountains or seashores through often monotonous but seldom disturbing surroundings. As John Steinbeck wrote in *Travels with Charley,* "When we get these thruways across the whole country, as we will and must, it will be possible to drive from New York to California without seeing a single thing." [4] Even if the superhighway did not yet make it possible to travel anywhere in the United States without seeing poverty in the 1950's, the airplane did. Indeed, the supersonic transport will make it possible to travel from New York to California without seeing anything but selected short subjects (or perhaps an occasional travelogue if passengers express an interest in knowing what the country over which they are flying is like).

The Increased Visibility of Poverty

If it were just a matter of growing suburbs and more rapid transportation, it would be easier to ignore poverty now than it was in the 1950's. But poverty is receiving increased attention today. Why has poverty all of a sudden become a cause of national concern?

One reason is the profit orientation of the American political parties and communications media. John Kennedy's success in gaining first the nomination of the Democratic Party and then election to the Presidency in 1960 after taking a stand against poverty led others to call attention to the same issue. Newspapers, magazines, and broadcasting networks recognized the possibility of large audiences for material on the subject. This does not mean that the politicians, editors, and producers were insincere in their efforts to call attention to the problem or in their demands for reform. Once the public is interested, profit reinforces concern. Expressions of concern then become more public and more frequent. These expressions of concern in turn stimulate greater public interest in the subject, and it becomes a topic of national debate.

A second reason for the growing awareness of poverty is the change that has taken place in the attitude of the poor themselves. From the early days of the Puritan settlement of New England through the laissez-faire period of the Nineteenth Century, poverty was looked upon as a sign of inferiority by those who were better off but also by a large percentage of the poor themselves. The poor were so because they were sinful or unfit or lazy. Since poverty was regarded as a sign of such an undeserving state, no one could claim that he had a right to a better

---

[4] John Steinbeck, *Travels with Charley in Search of America.* New York, N. Y.: The Viking Press, Inc., 1962.

economic position. Improvement could come about by an individual's showing that he was deserving through hard work or cleverness or from a gift of charity for which he was expected to be appropriately grateful. This attitude has undergone considerable change in recent years. More and more people, especially the poor themselves but also many who are not living in poverty, have come to look upon want not as a sign of individual inferiority but as a social illness which must be cured by the entire society. Conversely, they have come to look upon an adequate standard of living not as evidence of the virtue of the few but as the right of all Americans.

What has caused this change in attitude? Partly it is a result of the growth in size and complexity of the society. To the man in the city slum, surrounded by hundreds of thousands of others who are also badly off and isolated from those with adequate incomes who have moved from the city to the suburbs for a "better life," it is hard to see poverty as an individual condition. Partly it is the result of changes in industry. Many of the jobs that were traditionally used by hardworking but unskilled men as steppingstones toward a higher standard of living have disappeared. When these jobs were plentiful, an able-bodied man who was unemployed was likely to accept the idea that he had no one to blame but himself. As the jobs became scarcer and the man looking for work found none, he became more and more likely to blame society rather than himself for his condition.

Mass media, and especially television, have also helped to bring about this change in attitude. Adventure stories, family programs, and comedy hours all show Americans living the affluent life. This affluence is not presented as something unusual but rather as the "normal" way in which Americans live. Program after program presenting such a picture is interrupted only by commercials which describe luxury products which "everybody needs, deserves, and can easily afford." The poor are, in a sense, hit over the head with the idea that they are not sharing in the "normal" way of life which everyone "deserves." It should not be surprising that many should want their share.

The same change in attitude among the rural poor can also be traced to improved knowledge about what life is really like in the cities. Although there is still a steady flow of people from the farms to the cities, there is less of a tendency to look upon the latter as the "Promised Land" where all problems will automatically be solved.

A third reason for the rediscovery of poverty in the years since 1960 is the relationship between poverty and the problems of discrimination and race relations. Some would argue that racism is the real problem in America and that poverty is just one of its results. Others would argue that poverty is the real problem and that discrimination is the result. According to this second view, as long as there is not enough to go around, members of the majority group will rig the society in such a way as to assure themselves of all that they need. Many members of minority groups will thus have to do without, and the habits of poverty they develop will be used to justify continuation of the rigging.

Whichever argument is true, it is clear today that the problems of poverty and discrimination cannot be separated and that together they make an explosive mixture.

The seriousness of these problems was not acknowledged in the 1950's. Poverty, discrimination, and the like then led only to peaceful protests and demonstrations and to a slow rise in the tax rate as the costs of welfare payments increased. Demands for new programs that would cause dramatic increases in taxes brought some attention to the problem in the early '60's. But it was the series of riots which began in cities like Birmingham, Alabama, which spread to Chicago, Illinois, in 1963, and which became more serious in the Watts section of Los Angeles in the summer of 1965, that really awakened America. Looking at the destruction in Watts in 1965, some Americans feared that an insurrection might come. By the summer of 1967 many were convinced that the country was already in the middle of a full-scale revolution.

Interest in poverty has been awakened in the United States, but this does not mean that everyone agrees that it is an urgent problem. Some see it as the greatest challenge to the society. Others view it as a minor thing that has been blown up out of all proportion.

Those who see it as a great challenge are convinced of four things:

1. Poverty is no respecter of persons or places; it can strike any individual or group anywhere in the country.
2. There are tens of millions of people suffering from poverty throughout the country. Some of them are actually dying of starvation in an America that could easily afford to take proper care of them if it wished to do so.
3. Although the majority of those classed as poor in modern America may be better off than hundreds of millions of others around the world, their poverty is real and painful because it is in such marked contrast with the way of life of those in the mainstream of American affluence.
4. Poverty affects all Americans, not just those who are poor. It presents dangers to the economic prosperity, moral well-being, and physical security of the country.

Those who feel that the problem is being exaggerated counter that:

1. Poverty is a personal rather than a national problem because it affects only certain kinds of people who lack the strength to overcome it.
2. The estimates of the number of poor are far too high because they are based on dollar incomes. There are opportunities available to all so that there is no excuse for anyone's starving in America.

3. There will always be a lowest one-fifth or one-quarter of the population, no matter how well off they are, so the concern should be with their actual rather than relative standard of living.

4. Poverty is not the cause of, but only an excuse for, the rioting and other dangers that beset the nation.

Certainly there is no general agreement as to either the problem or the remedy. There is, however, active debate and a search for answers to questions that were not even being asked just a few years ago.

What Do You Think?

1. Will the United States ever be able to increase production enough so that everyone can have all that he wants, or will people always want more than they have?

2. Can you think of any other factors that may have contributed to the increased "visibility" of poverty today?

3. If you had to be poor, would you rather have most of the people around you poor also or better off? Why?

4. Does a country that is capable of producing plenty for all have a greater moral responsibility to fight poverty than a country that is not capable of doing so? Explain your reasoning.

ACTIVITIES FOR INVOLVEMENT

1. Write a description of the standard of living of an "average" American in the early colonial, Revolutionary, or Jacksonian period based on American history sources. Consider such things as food, clothing, shelter, transportation, entertainment, education, and governmental services. Then tell whether or not you would consider him poor and why.

2. Interview three or four adults who remember the Great Depression of the 1930's. Find out how it affected them personally. Write a report on the effects of the Depression on individuals based on your interviews.

3. There are a number of general statements concerning attitudes in the 1950's in this chapter. Ask your parents or other adults what they remember about this period and what their attitudes were then. How do they feel now about the period? Compare and contrast their answers with the general statements in the chapter. How would you explain the similarities and differences?

4. Conduct a poll among students outside your class and then among a sample of adults in your community as to whether or not they believe poverty is a serious problem in the United States today. Total the positive and negative responses which each group gives. How do the totals compare? How would you explain this?

Being Poor in
an Affluent Society

The problems of absolute poverty are easy to understand. The bony legs and arms, the distended stomach, and the haunted eyes of the child who is starving to death, whether on the main street of a city in India or hidden away in some corner of America, are easily recognized. There *are* people who suffer from such absolute poverty in the United States. The problems of the great majority of the poor in this affluent society, however, are much less easily comprehended. With either low-paying jobs or welfare funds available to them, most of the American poor do not display the traditional signs of total poverty: malnutrition and nakedness. They consume enough calories to appear well-fed, have enough clothing to appear "normal," and they even have a television set in the home. If the home itself is cramped, cold, and bare, it is probably also located somewhere out of the sight of most Americans.

If the poor in the American affluent society are so much better off than millions in Asia, Africa, and Latin America, why aren't they satisfied? Are there special problems that add to the miseries of poverty when it exists in the midst of a society of plenty?

One answer to this is, "No." Those who give this answer argue that there will always be a poorest group in any society, no matter how wealthy it may be, and that poor people who don't have the ability or ambition to rise up in the society should just be thankful that they live in a country that can take care of all so that they are not starving.

Others argue that if the American poor lived their lives in a vacuum many of them might easily be contented but that modern technology abhors such vacuums. Radios and television sets and means of rapid travel guarantee that the poor will be aware of the standard of living and of the expectations of the more affluent Americans. Commercials tell of products that everyone needs, deserves, and can easily afford. The poor are led to feel the need but know that they cannot afford the products. Programs describe a normal way of life in which there is freedom of choice of occupation, place of residence, and associates. The poor feel themselves trapped. Public service announcements point the way to a better future. "To get a good job, get a good education." The realities of education in poor areas have been effectively but disturbingly described in recent years.[1] Schools for the poor all too often offer little if any hope to those who attend them.

The readings in this chapter describe people who are hungry, people who have enough but nothing to spare, and people who are poor only in comparison with America's affluent majority. What is "being poor" like? Should all of these people be described as living in poverty?

1. 'LORD, I'M HUNGRY' *

Some of the worst poverty areas in America are located in rich farming regions. One such region is the so-called Black Belt, which touches Arkansas and Louisiana on the west and Georgia on the east. It also includes large portions of Mississippi and Alabama. Long a center of cotton production, it is fertile land. A large percentage of the population is black.

The reading below describes the conditions of the poor in the Mississippi Delta section of the Black Belt as of April, 1967.

Cleosa Henley just stood, a thick-shouldered, bullet-headed black ruin of 46, gazing dully out at the soybeans that have swallowed up his cotton rows, his garden patch and, very nearly, his life. Once, when cotton still was king in the Alabama Black Belt, it took 200 Negro tenant families to work Miss Nell Reed's plantation outside Boligee. Now, only a dozen remained in the surviving slapsided shacks, with little more than odd jobs or welfare to stave off starvation. Henley scratches up $30 a month loading timber when he's lucky, pays $10 a month rent for two cardboard-walled rooms and somehow stretches the rest into enough fat-

---

[1] Jonathan Kozol in *Death at an Early Age* (Boston, Mass.: Houghton Mifflin Company, 1967) describes his experiences in Boston schools. Bel Kaufman bases her novel *Up the Down Staircase* (Englewood Cliffs, N. J.: Prentice-Hall, Inc., 1964) on observations of the New York City school system.
* Copyright, *Newsweek,* Inc., July 24, 1967.

back, rice, grits, meal and greens to keep himself, his wife and seven kids alive. He can't remember the last time he ate meat, other than pig's ears, hog jowls or neck bones. Even relief costs money. Henley can buy $98 worth of Federal food stamps for $12—if he can ever put $12 together all at once. "I just ain't got that kinda money," says Henley, his gaze slowly dropping to his bare feet. "That money is right hard to git."

*   *   *   *   *

He is often hungry, indeed, to the point of slow starvation—and [he has] become a national issue. [In April, 1967,] a Senate antipoverty subcommittee chaired by Pennsylvania's Joseph Clark . . . toured the flat, rich bottom lands of the Mississippi Delta—and came back appalled at the sight of Negro children with all the marks of malnutrition: bloated bellies, drowsy eyes, runny sores. . . .

*   *   *   *   *

Hunger is not, of course, a Mississippi monopoly. It can be found anywhere cotton grows, or once grew. A half-mile or so off the highway, the shacks begin in all their uniform squalor: the leaky roofs, the wood sides weathered raw and rotten, the flies droning in through glassless, screenless windows, the outdoor privy, and the indoor walls plastered over with so many layers of newspaper and flour paste that they look like papier-maché.

*   *   *   *   *

FACES:

In one such shack, near Selma, Mrs. Florida Mae Andrew, 51, sits heavily in a rocker, starchy fat on a diet eked out of $20 a month for taking in washing, and sighs: "Lord, I'm so hungry I can't hardly stand up. But I got to go build a fire so's I can cook somethin'." In another, outside Greenville, Mississippi, hobbles Earl Jones—a shrunken, wrinkled man with a lame hip who is 36 and looks 50. He is one of the lucky ones: he takes home $20 a week as a tractor driver, a job not yet ground under by the new technology, and there is a pot of pinto beans simmering on the stove for dinner for his fourteen children. In still another shack, in Americus, Georgia, 12-year-old L. J. Crumbley, Jr., bubbles home from school with a spelling test he has just passed. The words— "meat," "soup," "lunch"—are abstractions: crippling rheumatism drove his father, an ex-sharecropper, off the land, and the family has no electricity, no water, no income, no hope.

*   *   *   *   *

A good many Negroes do leave for the towns of the south or the ghettoes of the north. "Chicago, Chicago—that's all you hear," says an ex-farm worker in the delta. But others stay—and struggle for bare existence. Thousands of Negroes subsist on free Federal foods such as grits, rice, flour—an eggless, fruitless, tasteless dole that was never meant to do more than supplement a family's regular diet. "You eat corn bread and beans every day of your life and it weaken you down," an Alabama tenant farmer says accurately.

---

1. There is much talk about diet in the article. Can a person's diet really affect his ability to earn a living? What evidence can you find to support your answer?

2. Twelve-year-old L. J. Crumbley, Jr., attends school. Is there anything in the article to indicate that education will lead to a better life for him? Explain.

3. How can the paradox of hunger existing in the midst of such rich farming land be explained?

2.   NO LIGHT AND NO GAS *

Next, a look at poverty in the northern city of Chicago, which is a frequent goal of those migrating from the rural south in an effort to escape from the ravages of poverty. In the selections below, poor people speak for themselves.

I haven't sufficient clothes to take my youngest to church on Sunday, but that's not the hardest thing about being poor. It's not having light or gas.

We used to be on relief, but my husband got a job two years ago and we were taken off. He can't take a day off from his job to go down and get help and he's the head of the house.

We have ten children and my husband works as a helper in a paper company. His take home pay is about $65 a week. That's not enough to support the family we got.

The gas and lights have been off for about seven months. We try to save up money for a deposit but we can't do it. It takes a $20 deposit when you've been shut off.

We use oil lamps and I am afraid to leave my children at home because of the oil lamps. One of us always has to be at home with the children no matter what. We buy the oil for 22 cents a gallon.

I cook on the coal heater that heats our apartment. It's large enough

---

to keep the place warm, but you can only cook one pot at a time. While I'm cooking one pot on the heater, I could be cooking my cornbread if we had a stove. We have rice, oatmeal, beans, peas, spaghetti, white potatoes and we have cornbread every day. The coal costs us 70 cents a bushel and we use two of them a day.

We don't have hot water and we got to heat the water too for washing up.

They charge us $50 a month rent for our 4 rooms. The children start at 2 months and go up to 14. We got three beds and a cot, where one child can sleep. Five of them sleep in one bed and four in the other.

We have to spend at least $30 a week for food. I have to get by on that. I have to stash the food away from the kids so it'll last the week, there's so many of them. I have two babies on the bottle and I have to have milk for them.

I've got to cook the meals every day on that heater. That's a big problem for me. I hope I get some light and gas on.

Shoes are a problem. Sometimes I go to the second-hand store and buy them shoes. But they don't stay in them. They don't hold. I have to buy shoes almost every week.

I have to buy pencils and books and paper and notebooks for the kids in school. I just have to stretch the check my husband brings home.

"Old People Have to Eat Well to Keep
Out of the Hospital"

It's too bad we older people are too old for sit-ins and demonstrations. Old people have to eat well to keep out of the hospital. But how can they do it on $9 a week?

Each month I get $50.40 from the government as my husband's army pension. He was gassed in the First World War and died in 1928. The welfare was giving me $29 a month to supplement it. Then last year, they took $3 off of that. What I don't understand is how they can do that with prices going up and all. I guess it's just one of those things you don't understand.

In June I'll be 78. I think you should be thankful you have lived that long.

My rent is $40 a month. We have five tenants in this flat. The others each have one of the bedrooms. I have the living room because it is cheaper since there aren't any closets. I use the hall closet.

After I've paid the $40, I have $36 to eat and live on for the month. I have diverticulitis [a disease of the colon]. I have to eat six meals a day and there are many foods I have to eat and many I can't. That both hurts and helps the budget.

Every once in a while a church member brings me a chicken and a dollar or two, but I'm getting desperate.

Today I have to go down to Sears to buy a brace for my back. A friend told me to take her charge plate and then I can give her something on it every once in a while.

The shoes I have on were given to me. They hurt the woman's feet who bought them. I have been very fortunate. I have not had to buy a pair in over a year and a half.

But when people are so nice, you feel so obligated. The biggest thing I'd like is to be to myself.

I haven't been to my church for a long time. And I feel so bad I haven't been able to give them any dues. But the church members bring me Communion every first Sunday and they say it is all right because a lot of people can't pay any dues.

I've sold everything I had. I had a beautiful pair of earrings my husband gave me and a fur coat and rings. There is nothing left to sell.

The only piece of furniture I own here is that small bed over there. A friend of mine that worked at a convent got it for me when the sister there got a new one. So, you're looking at something holy.

I'm supposed to drink a quart of milk a day. I get powdered milk. I don't like it but they tell me it is as good for me as fresh milk so I drink it anyway. I think it costs me 79 cents a package and that makes about 2½ gallons.

The way they want me to eat (six meals a day) would take a stick of margarine each day. If you don't eat that, there ain't no need to go to the doctor. It's just a question of insufficient diet.

Meat is very expensive. I have to get very good hamburger because the cheap stuff makes me sick. I get ground beef. It costs 69 cents a pound so I make it into little patties and put them into the refrigerator. I eat about a pound and a half a week. Some meals I just eat eggs because they are just as good for me. Fish and ham are too expensive.

Sweet potatoes, they are not the best, but sometimes you can get a can of them for 10 cents. I watch on carrots, green beans, peas and beets for when they are on sale. Then I get them. I usually get two or three meals out of a can.

Every once in a while I get me a little 10 cent package of cake mix and make me a little cake or a little jello mix and make some jello.

I smoke, but I get two or three lights out of a cigarette. I have a smoke and put it out and then light it up again. I don't inhale. Somehow, it's company for me. I can just sit and smoke and look out the window and think up more things.

I miss company. I feel kind of forgotten. My church members are kind of old and don't like climbing three flights of stairs.

When I go to the doctor's, I can walk over three blocks and catch the South Parkway bus and I don't have to buy a transfer, but when it's bad I catch the Indiana bus which goes in front of my door.

I do my laundry in the bathtub. You can get three bars of Ivory soap for 29 cents or American Family soap for 31 cents.

I haven't had any new clothes since when. Back when I did buy my clothes, fortunately they were good ones and lasted. My suit needs a cleaning, but it's four years old. I would like a new winter coat. After wearing it seven years and being a woman, you would like a new one. But it's all right.

We have a telephone and I have to tell the truth. I don't always put the dime there. I just go back and use it.

If I see a sale on toothpaste, I'll buy it. If I don't have the money, I'll just buy baking soda. I gargle with salt water. What I should have are some teeth. But when these are bad, I just take them out and rest my gums.

I stopped sending Christmas cards years ago. I beat that racket. But I do write a lot of letters. A young girl I know gets stamps from work and I get mine from her. I think the only official I haven't written is Mayor Daley.

My medicine I get free at the clinic, but I have to take a bus to go get it. Somebody told me that if it is really bad you can take a cab and they will pay for it. I will have to check that with my welfare worker.

Some people ask me why don't I get a live-in job. But I can't because there's some days I just don't feel like moving.

I worked for years at resorts at French Lick, Indiana, and at Warm Springs, but it always seemed like they'd tell me there wasn't enough people working there for me to pay social security, so I never got it.

The rent has not gone up in the nine years I've lived here, but still I have to do something about it. If I could just have an efficiency apartment in public housing! But to get into that housing you have to have a mouthpiece. I applied at the office at Cermak and State last September and got a letter telling me that my registration number was 176,561— how far down the list can you get?

If I was in politics, I would have a mouthpiece and I would be pushed up on the list and cheat somebody else. I could go to Mayor Daley, but I figure he's building them so he figures it's up to you to get into them.

I'm not used to being old. I get tired and out of breath easily, especially climbing those stairs. I have a little heart trouble and it just seems I'm ailing all the time.

I want to keep as active as I can, but I think this worrying about things is affecting my memory as bad as old age is.

What Do You Think?

1.   There are people in other parts of the world who are worse off than these. Is Mr. Heise justified in calling these people who are speaking destitute?

2.   The old woman says, "The biggest thing I'd like is to be to myself." What does she mean? How important is this for people?

3.   Are there some items of food that are more expensive for these people than they are for others who are better off? Explain.

4.   The poor people in these readings frequently speak of things that they plan to do or questions that they plan to ask. Do you think they will ever actually do these things? What evidence can you find in the selections to support your answer?

3.   WILL THE PICKERS COME? *

Some of the poor live in the rural south and others in the urban north. There are still others who do not have permanent homes at all. These are the migrants. They are mostly farm workers who move around the country finding work wherever it is available and existing somehow when no work can be found. The following selection describes the homes and travels of typical migrant families.

Every spring the Fontanez family and other thousands fan out from the southwest in search of work in crops.

A minority of them migrate entirely inside the state they call home. There are a few states where, during every month of the year, one crop or another demands hand labor. A California migrant cycle may go from winter cotton to Imperial Valley vegetables, then on to San Joaquin apricots to peaches to beans to tomatoes to Fresno grapes, and meet itself again in fall and winter cotton. Within Texas, cotton picking begins in July in the Rio Grande Valley and moves up the coast to central Texas; the harvest comes to a climax in the Panhandle in October and then dwindles through west Texas to a December end; meantime in the lower Rio Grande Valley and that fabulous sector that calls itself the

* Excerpted from Louisa R. Shotwell, *The Harvesters: The Story of the Migrant People*. Copyright © 1961 by Louisa R. Shotwell. Reprinted by permission of Doubleday & Company, Inc.

Winter Garden there is vegetable and citrus harvest in winter and on through spring and early summer.

But most Spanish American migrants cross a score or more of state lines in the course of a crop season. Some start out from New Mexico or Arizona or California or Colorado. Those from Texas, where the greatest number have some kind of home base, are found during a single year working in thirty-two states.

Such are the hazards of weather, blight, market slumps, labor surplus, and time eaten up in travel and job hunting that if there exists a migrant who has found work for any fifty-two consecutive weeks, either within a single state or across the country, nobody has tracked him down.

Migrants may or may not return to home base for the winter. One Texas Mexican family turned up in the central New York State bean harvest four years after leaving the Texas community they still speak of as home. For some, home base is a house of their own somewhere across the tracks in the Mexican quarter of a southwestern town. Manuel Fontanez' wooden unpainted three rooms in the *colonia* of Crescent City was built by the family themselves on a thirty-foot square plot. To get the land they paid ten dollars down and a dollar a month whenever the man came around to collect. (Finally he stopped coming, and in time they heard he had moved to California.)

The house has in each room one glass window and one naked electric light bulb; it has an old-fashioned icebox only rarely containing ice but convenient for storing staples, an outdoor water faucet shared by half a dozen neighbors, a porch with two front doors, and a market value of eight hundred dollars. It does not trouble the Fontanezes that they have no deed to the property. They know it is theirs, and it does not occur to them that their possession of it may be threatened.

Some families consider their home a cabin in a distant migrant labor camp, the door padlocked against their return. For others the symbol of home is no more than the mental image of a camp where they have been before and to which they hope sometime to go back, with no padlock and no cabin designated in their own minds or anybody else's as theirs; everything they own in the world journeys with them as they follow the crops by truck or jalopy. Still others make no pretense at having a home base of any kind.

Some follow a familiar pattern from season to season, returning year after year to the same growers. Some, like the Fontanezes, travel in small immediate family groups; others move with families expanded by relatives of relatives to forty or fifty or seventy-five. Still others may be members of very much larger crews impersonally assembled afresh every season by labor contractors. More likely than not these never know by name or face the owner of the crop they are working in; they work not for Mr. Johnson or Mr. Brown or Mr. Van Leyden; they work in cherries or cotton or on the beans. Indeed, the odds are increasingly good that the owner is not a man at all but a corporation. Many Spanish Americans prefer the smaller groups. They set great store by their personal relationship with the farmer; the opportunity to identify themselves with his interests attracts them more than does work in a large-scale operation in which they feel no real sense of participation.

Unknown numbers set forth without a known destination, depending on roadside signs of "Tomato Pickers Wanted" or on newspaper displays asking for peach thinners or radio voices pleading for almond knockers. Or they count on that mystical instrument, the migrant grapevine, to tell them where sugar beets or broccoli or potatoes or carrots or lettuce may need extra hands for hoeing or thinning or harvesting.

The more knowledgeable among the family heads make contact with Farm Placement offices, affiliates of the United States Employment Service maintained in an attempt to perform the staggering role of mustering enough and not too many workers in the right place at the right time. Others shun these offices because Farm Placement personnel seem to smack of government authority and because they ask questions: in Latin-American minds questions from anybody in authority too often symbolize a prelude to jail. The Fontanezes share this fear of authority; they keep a healthy distance from employment offices. As a result, they have more than once had the disquieting experience of hearing that three hundred workers are needed in a particular crop, only to arrive there in company with droves of others like them to find that the three hundred jobs have been filled by workers recruited through employment service channels. Yet it takes more than half a dozen such incidents to dissipate their dread of formal face-to-face dealings with officials.

The eight-hundred-mile leg of the Fontanez journey to Missouri is a short one compared to some. The initial trek may carry them all the way to Idaho for potatoes, or to Wisconsin for asparagus or cherries, or to Michigan for sugar beets or blueberries. A good number of Texas Mexicans head first for Oregon, where laborers of Spanish American ancestry are welcomed for the early sugar beet and onion work because they are "accustomed to stoop labor and have for years engaged in this work." South Dakota acknowledges its indebtedness to them for the arduous weeding and thinning of 5300 acres of sugar beets, a harvest need that in this state lasts from mid-May to mid-July.

Some of the Latin crews (they prefer this euphemism, for they have learned from experience the opprobrium that attaches to the word "Mexican") make straight for the state of Washington, a northwest journey from south Texas upward of twenty-four hundred miles, where seasonal harvest needs extend from April to October and reach their peak in June. For this trip the customary departure time is three in the morning, allowing a day and a night to Las Cruces, New Mexico, another day and night across Arizona to Blythe, California, and a third twenty-four hour lap to carry them to Washington.

What Do You Think?

1.   The man from whom the Fontanez family obtained its lot did not give them a deed and apparently just stopped collecting for it and moved to California. How can these actions be be explained?

2.   Is this need to be on the move all the time a sign of poverty? How else might you explain their constant travelling?

3.   Can anyone who owns his own home be considered poor? Explain.

4.   How would you explain the attitude towards people in authority which migrants display? Is there any relationship between this attitude and poverty? Explain.

4.   DISPATCH FROM WOUNDED KNEE *

If there are some of America's poor who have no homes of their own, there are others descended from people who once were able to call the entire land theirs.

The Pine Ridge Indian Reservation in South Dakota is the home of nearly 10,000 American Indians. The article which follows describes the condition of reservation Indians who are neither the richest nor the poorest in the country. To what extent does reservation life illustrate conditions of poverty and deprivation?

U. S. Highway 18 passes east-west through the southern edge of the reservation. There are miles and miles of good blacktop roads kept in repair by Indians working for the Interior Department road service; and there are miles and miles of roads that are no good at all. There are modern boarding schools exclusively for Indian children as well as local public schools and a Catholic mission school, outlying clinics and a good free hospital with doctors, surgeons, dentists and a psychiatrist. There are churches of all kinds (40 per cent of the Indians profess to be Catholics and more to be Protestants, but the old beliefs still lie heavily in their souls). There is an American Legion Post, a Lions Club, a Ladies' Aid, a P.-T. A. and a Boy Scout troop. Nearly all of the Sioux (or Dakotas, their own pre-reservation name for themselves) speak English as well as

---

* By Calvin Kentfield, *The New York Times Magazine,* October 15, 1967. © 1967 by The New York Times Company. Reprinted by permission.

their native Lakota dialect, and there are still a few medicine men around, like old Frank Fools Crow who usually presides over the annual Sun Dance. The center of nearly everything—government, society, law and order, education—is Pine Ridge, a town of 1,256 people close enough to the state line to have a "suburb" in Nebraska, Whiteclay, center of shopping (three supermarkets) and entertainment (bars and dance halls).

On this reservation live, in one fashion or another, nearly 10,000 Teton Sioux of the Oglala tribe. They are not the poorest nor the richest of the country's Indians. The Hopis and some of the Apaches of the Southwest are poorer, and the inhabitants of the Aguacaliente reservation in Southern California, who more or less own Palm Springs, are richer, to say nothing of those few tribes that have oil wells. But the Oglalas range from a state of imminent starvation to fair affluence.

On the reservation itself, unemployment is 43 per cent, so some of the younger people go elsewhere for summer work. There is a new factory at Pine Ridge that employs about a hundred people to make "handmade" moccasins. A fishhook factory near Wounded Knee employs nearly 200 more, and a few more work for the Bureau of Indian Affairs. Most of the businesses—filling stations, grocery stores—are owned by whites, and the rest of the Indians work for white ranchers or live off the land which they work themselves or lease to white ranchers. The land, though it belongs to the Indians, is held in trust by the Department of the Interior, which takes care of all the leasing arrangements and issues checks to the owners each month from a computer in Aberdeen.

*   *   *   *   *

"We try to help them," said Brice Lay in his office in the new air-conditioned [Bureau of Indian Affairs] headquarters in Pine Ridge, "to make the best possible use of the land they have, but it's very hard." Like most of the non-Indian (the bureau does not use the term "white man") employes of the bureau, he is intensely sincere in his desire to help the Indian become a white man. "Here in Pine Ridge most of the people live fairly well, but you go out on the reservation—the way some of those people live!" He made a gesture of despair. "No one should have to live that way."

And, indeed, out on the windy treeless tracts of the reservation, at the end of two dirt ruts across the prairie, will be a one-room shack, possibly a log cabin, possibly a frame house walled in tarpaper, for a family of six, eight, ten people and surrounded by a circle of old car bodies that, like the bodies of U. S. soldiers killed in a battle of olden times, have been stripped and mutilated and left to rot where they lay. An outhouse nearby. No electricity, no running water. A monthly ration of rice, flour, powdered milk, peanut butter, margarine, lard, raisins, oatmeal, cornmeal, potted meat, dried beans, dried peas, bulgar and rolled wheat, plus $50 in cash from Welfare. This kind of poverty engenders horror, pity and disgust in the Anglo-Saxon breast, but all the Oglalas are not that badly off, and many of them simply don't want some of the amenities that the Great White Father insists they must have, if possible, for their own good.

"We have one old woman out on the reservation," Brice Lay said, "that was all by herself and living in a tent, so we found a house for her, but she wouldn't move in. She said she'd die if she lived in a house, that the air in a house was bad air. Oh, she was stubborn. But finally," he concluded with a tone of great satisfaction, "we got her in there."

Out at Wounded Knee about two miles from the general store and post office lives a man in his late 50's, his wife, two married sons, six grandchildren, three dogs, two cats, some hens and a rooster. He is a full blood, very dark, though his wife is not. He owns a section of land (640 acres) through which runs Wounded Knee Creek and on which graze about 200 head of cattle and 60 or 70 horses. He has a field of alfalfa which, this year, because of the late rains, is exceptionally rich and high and, when I visited him, was ready for cutting. There are tall shade trees along the creek, plenty of water, and a small field of sweet corn nearby.

He and his wife and one orphaned grandchild live in a very old, one-room log cabin with a shade, or "squaw cooler" (though "squaw" is an insulting word these days), a kind of summer house made of poles and pine boughs that keep off the sun but let the breeze come through, making it a comfortable outdoor kitchen and sleeping place during the hot months. His sons and their families live in small asphalt-shingled houses on either side of the parental house. One son is a cowboy and works the section, the other works at the fishhook factory over the hill. Standing to one side at the edge of the alfalfa is a two-hole outhouse.

They carry their water from the creek, build their fire with wood and light their lamps with kerosene. They walk to the store and back, as they have no car. They are well and presumably happy. They are members of the Native American Church who use peyote, the hallucinatory cactus, in their services, during which, under the spell of the drug, they chant and sing and pray to God that the day will come when all men will be at peace and all men will be brothers. Not half a mile from this man's house reside the bones in a mass hilltop grave of the victims of the massacre of Wounded Knee.

What Do You Think?

1. Was the last family described, the one that lived near the Wounded Knee battleground, living in poverty? Explain the standards that you are using to determine whether or not poverty exists.

2. Was it a compliment to Brice Lay to describe him as a man who was "intensely sincere in his desire to help the Indian become a white man"? How would an Indian respond to this idea? Explain.

3. Compare the descriptions of poverty found in this reading with those in the other readings in this chapter. In what ways is the poverty similar? In what ways different? How can you explain the similarities and differences?

5. LIFE ON WELFARE:
A DAILY STRUGGLE FOR EXISTENCE *

The city equivalent of the Indian agent is the welfare worker. The welfare departments in the big cities hire experts whose job it is to determine exactly what a family or an individual needs to maintain life in the city and how much these things cost. The number of razor blades needed per year by the employed man, the number of bars of soap needed per person per year, the amount of deodorant for an unemployed woman, all are computed and used to determine the amount to be paid to welfare clients. No one, then, who is eligible for welfare aid needs to do without any of those things which the experts feel are absolutely necessary, and so no one needs to suffer from absolute poverty conditions. If absolute poverty is not the problem of the welfare client, then, what is? The next reading describes life on welfare in New York City.

It was 6:30 in the morning and the Pressley family—Ruth Pressley and her six children—started moving about their Harlem apartment in a swift, although sleepy-eyed, routine of getting ready for school.

An ancient radio, with an uncovered speaker, sputtered and buzzed as it gave out time signals, commercials, music and news.

"Get that big O. K. for cash today," a jingle blared on behalf of a loan company.

"It's 6:45, Ruthie," Mrs. Pressley called to her 16-year-old daughter, repeating a time check. "Come out of that bathroom."

Then in quick succession the radio listeners were urged to both "See the Dodge boys, today" and "Jet Delta to Birmingham" before another time signal was called.

"Sharon," Mrs. Pressley called to another daughter, "It's 6:54; is that oatmeal on?"

Mrs. Pressley, a 45-year-old, raw-boned, deliberate woman says she does not "hear" many of the morning commercials.

---

* By Thomas A. Johnson, *The New York Times,* December 19, 1966. © 1966 by The New York Times Company. Reprinted by permission.

While some people screen out commercials by choice, the Pressleys do it out of necessity, out of defense. This family is on relief and like more than 655,000 of New York's poorest, they survive in the backwash of the city's mainstream.

Many goods and services considered normal for most people must be acquired at a sacrifice for welfare recipients or forgotten. Two bus fares, for instance, or a package of cigarettes could take half of the daily food allotment of about 90 cents for a family member who eats at home. And a single person, authorized to eat in restaurants, could not buy a ticket to some first-run movies with his daily food grant of $2.50.

"I listen to some commercials about detergents," Mrs. Pressley told a visitor recently as she chased roaches from the breakfast table. "I want to see what they say about getting clothes clean."

While she washed the table, a cheery voice on the radio proclaimed: "Oh, yes, things are great in Ford country."

To observe public assistance from the recipients' point of view, this reporter for The New York Times lived recently with families on relief and also in a furnished room in a residence hotel that houses mostly single welfare clients.

Many clients, because of their age, an illness, lack of training, or discrimination, were found to have no hope of joining the more affluent majority.

Despair and cynicism shape much of their thinking.

For many, cheating "the system" has become a way of life, a survival technique.

For the Pressleys that morning's breakfast was simply oatmeal and tea. There have been times, Mrs. Pressley said, when the children had no breakfast at all.

Susan Pressley, who is 7 years old, said she would like some corn flakes for breakfast as she waited for an older sister, Mary, who is 11, to finish using a cereal bowl.

Mrs. Pressley promised to buy corn flakes ("not the sugared kind— they cost too much") when the welfare check arrived.

"That's one reason why I went to work," Mrs. Pressley explained, "so I could have a little more money for my family. It's not much more, though, and it doesn't go very far when you add up the carfare and cleaning bills and such."

Before she went to work in July as a part-time neighborhood aide for the Urban League's Open City program that promotes housing desegregation, Mrs. Pressley had received $184 twice a month from the Welfare Department. The department now deducts her weekly salary ($30) from the welfare allowance but adds employment expenses (carfare, lunch, clothes, cleaning bills, etc.) so that her combined income now comes to $203 twice a month.

"I also want the children to see me working, too—to see that life is more than waiting for a government check," she said.

In an informal accounting, Mrs. Pressley estimated that her monthly expenditures were: food, $150; rent, $111; clothing, $20; gas and electricity, $15; cost for care of her son, Christopher, 3, while she works, $52; employment expenses, $20; household supplies, $7; laundry, $7; personal items, $12; school expenses, $5 and roach killer, $4. The total: $403.

"We buy chickens a lot and pork roasts, fish, or stew beef—whatever is cheap on check day," Mrs. Pressley said. She said it was not possible to save for a movie. "There's never enough."

Mrs. Pressley came to New York from Roanoke, Va., in the early nineteen-forties. She worked as a streetcar conductor during World War II and later as a 35-cent-an-hour domestic and factory worker. Her first contact with the Welfare Department, she said, was about 16 years ago. Since then she has received public assistance "off and on," the last time starting about three years ago after a separation from her husband. He is disabled now, she said, and lives in Brooklyn, also on public assistance.

During the years, Mrs. Pressley said, she has not developed any particular pattern of dealing with case workers. "They change too often," she said. "By the time we get to know one another, the investigator's been changed."

Mrs. Pressley is suspicious of the whole welfare system, noting that millions of dollars are spent, but clients "receive so little."

"Somebody must be stealing like mad down there," she said half joking.

Mrs. Pressley said that in the past, when she tried to work while on welfare, things did not go smoothly.

"Once, I was working and I told the investigator not to call the employer and that I would show him my pay receipt as proof. He called my boss to check and I was fired the same day—many people don't want clients working for them."

Another time, Mrs. Pressley said she had worked as a nurse's aid for four months and her case worker failed to record the income. "Suddenly they closed my case and they said I was indicted for grand larceny for concealing my income, but the judge threw the case out of court."

"The case was closed for a long time and I got desperate," she said. "I put on a tight skirt and a lot of make-up and went to a bar on Lenox Avenue. But the bartender said: 'You're no prostitute, what're you doing here?' I told him, and he gave me a couple of dollars and told me to go to the police station the next day. The police gave me a box of food."

The Pressley household, where the children range from 3 to 16, does not have bicycles, toys, coloring books or comic books. It is, for the most part, a household of functional objects needed for a semblance of modern-day survival. But even these, the broken beds and dressers, the unmatched chairs and tables, have all served other households before.

But the furnishings are hardly Mrs. Pressley's biggest worry.

"He doesn't talk about it, but I know my son would like to go to the movies with his friends," she said. "And my daughters, they would like to be able to buy stylish clothes. They don't talk about these things but I know they would like to do them."

A visitor to the Pressley apartment steps into a long, dimly lit hallway, covered with dark green paint. Rusty stains from broken water pipes show through the paint on the upper floors.

The apartment is kept very clean and despite a continuing battle against them, roaches climb the walls, walk the floors and invade dressers and closets.

"I guess we spend about a dollar a week on roach killer insecticides," Mrs. Pressley said, "but they always come back. They live in the walls and under the floors. They always come back."

Craig Pressley, who is 14, warned a visitor recently that a roach had crawled on top of the visitor's shoe. "Kill it," Craig said.

The visitor dislodged the insect but missed in a clumsy attempt to smash it. A young neighbor did the job, expertly, with his foot.

*   *   *   *   *

[There are many people on public assistance or welfare who are even worse off.]

There are thousands of aged persons who live as frightened recluses in what are known as single room occupancy accommodations, many on the West Side. Here, however, a good percentage of the aged are white and were left alone when their children moved from the city to the suburbs. They spend much of their time waiting for visits from their children. When the weather is good they crowd the benches on Broadway's center mall. Welfare laws require children to support their parents if they are able to and some received money from their children.

Since World II these elderly persons have been joined by thousands of disabled and low-salaried non-whites and in the poorer serviced "residence hotels," many live in their cell-like cubicles in constant and often justified fear of marauding drug addicts, drunks, and petty criminals.

Facilities at many of these buildings are dehumanizing at best. In many cases they are unhealthy and unsafe.

Kitchen and bathroom facilities in these buildings are shared.

One woman, disabled by a cardiac condition, said: "I used to clean up the bathroom every day, but then other people, nasty people from all the other floors, used to troop to this bathroom because it was clean. Then they would mess it up. I only clean for myself now."

Another woman said there were no locks on the bathroom doors and tenants sing or talk while using the facilities. Locks, she said, had been placed on the bathroom doors but visitors or addicts, who did not have keys, broke them.

The dehumanizing conditions in these buildings is matched, perhaps, only by the ability of landlords to utilize every inch of space. Thus, dumbwaiter shafts have been plugged and are used as closets. Closets have been converted into tiny kitchens. These kitchens hold a small refrigerator with a two-burner hotplate on top of the refrigerator. Completing the arrangement is a kitchen cabinet—an orange crate nailed to the wall.

Garbage receptacles consist of a large tin or cardboard drum (or sometimes just a burlap bag), in the hallway. But infrequent collection by the superintendent has a predictable result: a garbage strewn hallway, a condition that inevitably attracts rats.

"They are never emptied on the weekends," said one elderly relief client-pensioner, retired a few years ago after working for 40 years in the garment district. "On the weekends you can't even get to the stairs for the garbage on the floor."

"I keep my garbage inside my room at night if I forget to put it out earlier," said Mrs. Ursela Brazer, who receives public assistance for herself and her 7-year-old daughter at the Pendleton Hotel. . . .

Although such single room occupancy buildings are officially only supposed to have one person a room, many house women with children because it is difficult for the Welfare Department to find places for its clients.

A native of the Virgin Islands, Mrs. Brazer said most of the women tenants she knew opened their doors only during daylight hours. "Many bums walk in and out of the house," she said. "They often knock on the doors at night."

Other night sounds include the thud of garbage bags when they land in courtyards. Some tenants admit dispatching refuse "by air mail." They fear being mugged in dark or unlit hallways at night; they are afraid rats will crawl into their rooms if they keep garbage.

*   *   *   *   *

But the major problem of the welfare recipient is living on the welfare grant.

A South Bronx mother complained: "You want to be the same as people who are not on relief, but you just can't do it. You never have enough money—I don't know what to do."

Another mother on welfare admitted finding a solution. Young and attractive, she walked recently along Columbus Avenue near 81st Street and in a low voice asked men if they were interested in "some sport." She admitted later to "tricking" in order to earn extra money. But, she explained, she never operated "close to where I live, or around people I know."

Another welfare recipient was not so circumspect. Asked by school officials why her children sometimes went to sleep in class, the mother said that sometimes she kept them outside the apartment until late at night.

"I have to do business if they're going to eat," she said.

While welfare budgets are computed to cover a variety of needs, most recipients say they can pay only the essential bills—rent, gas and electricity—while the remainder is spent for food.

A 48-year-old woman who came to the Lower East Side 10 years ago from Puerto Rico, and worked steadily until she was disabled by diabetes three years ago, finds that she often must depend on handouts from friends or live on bread and coffee.

Her twice monthly check is $35.40. Her rent is $23.40 a month. Gas and electricity costs about $17 every two months. The remainder is spent on food.

"There is never enough food for the full two weeks and never even enough for a pair of stockings," she said.

The woman said she had been given a winter coat by the Welfare Department but it was stolen and her case worker is so overworked she cannot take time to comply with the various departmental procedures required to have the garment replaced.

The recipient wears a neighbor's coat to visit the Lower Manhattan Welfare Center every few days to inquire about the replacement. She says she could not leave her house if her neighbor decided to go outdoors on the same day

The checks that welfare recipients receive twice each month set in motion a predictable series of events.

It starts with the mailman.

Mailboxes in many slum buildings no longer protect their contents from theft. Long ago their locks were broken and their panels smashed. As a result, checks are either handed to waiting recipients or left with landlords or building superintendents.

Flanked by guards, many landlords sit inside barred rooms where they cash welfare checks and issue rent receipts.

Later, the salesmen arrive with thick account books and the ability to deliver almost anything a welfare recipient wants (for a signature). They hustle in and out of the buildings where recipients live collecting a payment here and selling a new item there. Their pattern, like that of many appliance and furniture stores selling goods on time to unemployed welfare recipients, is to collect as much of the debt as possible and repossess the item if payments stop.

While a few of the welfare recipients descend on supermarkets for provisions on check day, most hurry to small, neighborhood grocers. Prices are higher in the smaller stores, and there is less of a selection. But the neighborhood grocer extends credit during the lean days.

An assistant state attorney general said price gouging of welfare recipients—from overpriced appliances to supermarkets raising prices on check day—were "commercial facts of life."

"Most supermarkets will not admit it," said the state official, Joseph Bailey, "but some do raise their prices on check day. Some do it to offset the cost of hiring guards who patrol the stores against pilferage."

A spokesman for the New York State Retail Food Merchants Association denied such a pattern on the part of "reputable supermarkets."

"They're all competing for the dollar and will keep their prices as low as they can," the spokesman said.

The arrival of checks during the day also brings problems at night.

The police have noted that there is an upsurge of violent crimes on check night. They also think that many incidents probably go unreported.

"We get a lot of drunks rolled, a lot of pocketbooks and sometimes groceries snatched and some muggings," a Police Department spokesman said. "Many alkys (alcoholics) get taken over and over again."

Parties, or "check gigs," are sometimes thrown by recipients in celebration of their twice-monthly incomes. Questioned about a recent West Side "gig," the hostess said she liked the music, the drinks, and the people.

"Don't you give parties?" she asked.

What Do You Think?

1. Mrs. Pressley tells of things she knows her children want but do not talk about. Why don't they talk about them?
2. Would most of the problems of the welfare recipients be solved if they spent their check money more wisely?
3. If you had to be on welfare, which of the following would bother you the most: shortage of food and clothing, doing without things you knew most Americans had, the way other people look down on welfare clients, or the hopelessness of the situation?
4. What answer would you have given the welfare recipient who, when asked why she gave parties, responded by asking, "Don't you give parties?"
5. Does poverty endanger family life? Explain.

ACTIVITIES FOR INVOLVEMENT

1. Take an outline map of the United States and draw in the areas of poverty described in the selections in this chapter. As other areas are described in later chapters or in your research or class discussions, add them to the map.

2. Review all the selections included in this chapter. What evidence can you find to indicate that poverty is not restricted to any one section of the country, any one setting, or any one group of people? Write a "Letter to the Editor" responding to an editorial entitled, "All Poor People Are Alike."

3. Prepare a written research report on the history of a specific area of poverty. Your paper should include such things as:
    a. The location and description of the area.
    b. A description of the people who live there.
    c. The economic history of the area: Has it ever been poor?
    d. The causes of poverty in the area.
    e. What is being done and what can be done to overcome poverty.

4. Listen to a morning "time, music, and news" type program for half an hour. List all the announcements and commercials that a family like the Pressley's would have to "screen out."

5. Mrs. Pressley can spend about $150 a month on food. This is approximately $5 a day. Using actual prices in a supermarket or listed in newspaper advertisements, prepare a complete menu for a family of seven for one day for $5. To what extent does this menu represent poverty?

6. Compare the lives of the different groups of poor people in this chapter. Which is worse—to be poor in the country or in the city? To have a miserable home or no home at all? Explain your reasoning.

7. If you had $1,000 you wished to give away, to which of the people described in this chapter would you give it? Defend your choice.

What Causes Poverty?

4

In earlier societies it was easy to explain the presence of poverty. There just wasn't enough to go around and so some people had to do without. It is not so easy to explain in an affluent society where there is more than enough to go around.

How can poverty in America today be explained then? There are several possible ways. There are those who argue that it exists because there are some people in the society who are too lazy or too lacking in character to take care of themselves. There are others who argue that it is the result of historical or economic forces beyond the power of man to control. Others see the root of poverty in discrimination and say that poverty exists because the well-to-do want it to exist. Some see it as the result of unwise actions that the government has taken. Finally, there are those who see it as different in every case and argue that we must look at the poor as individuals and find the unique set of causes for their poverty.

Which are the correct explanations? Or is it possible that all are partly correct? What does cause poverty?

1. "WHY SHOULD THEY WORK WHEN THEY CAN GET WELFARE?" *

There are many people who see lack of ambition or weakness of character on the part of the poor themselves as the primary causes

---

* A composite of two discussions held in a social studies class in Sleepy Hollow High School, North Tarrytown, N. Y.

of poverty. There were several students who felt this way in the social studies class in which the following exchange took place.

The class was in the middle of a discussion of current news. Tony had just reported hearing an item on a local radio station. Officials were predicting a sharp rise in county taxes.

Sally: "That makes three, then, the income tax, the state tax, and this; all going up."

Teacher: "Does the idea bother you?"

Sally: "Well, sure. The way things are going, we're all going to be working for the government pretty soon. Taxes are too high already. They ought to lower them rather than raise them. I mean, we can't afford taxes like these."

Al: *(Interrupting)* "You don't pay 'em."

Sally: "You know what I mean. My parents do and that affects me. I mean, my parents pay them and that's less than they can spend for college and other things for me."

Teacher: "Do many of you really have to do without things you need because of taxes?"

(Silence and some looking around)

Tony: "It's not so much that. It's that the government wastes most of the money."

Teacher: "Really?"

Tony: "Maybe not 'most,' but a lot."

Frank: "You know that whenever the government does something it costs more. Every politician has to get something out of it."

Mary Louise: "Never say, 'Every.' "

Frank: "O.K., O.K."

Art: "Anyway, the thing that really takes a lot of the money and makes the taxes go up is the welfare. We wouldn't need any of these tax increases, except maybe the national one, if they'd make everybody on welfare go to work."

Teacher: "Are there many people on welfare who are able to work who aren't?"

Several students: "Yes!"

Teacher: "How do you know?"

Frank: "My father has been trying to hire a man to clean up at his shop. He's gone down to the state employment office lots of times. He's talked to some of the welfare men there and had a couple who came up here. They don't want to work. They make up some sort of excuses when they learn what kind of work it is. Sure, maybe if you offered them a nice desk job at $20,000 a year and no real work they'd be glad to take it. But when they learn that he wants them to clean up they say they've got bad backs or can't get transportation or don't want to be too far from home. One guy drove up in a big Buick—my father saw him—but when he learned he'd have to sweep the floors he said he didn't have any way to get to the job. My father asked him, 'What about that Buick?' and he said, 'Oh, I just borrowed it.' He probably owns it and is paying for it with his welfare money."

Mary Louise: "We've had the same trouble trying to get a cleaning lady. You ask them to do some ironing because there isn't enough cleaning to take the whole day and they say, 'Oh, I'm not supposed to do that.' Then, if my mother insists, she does a careless job and then the next week calls up and says she's sick. You try to make them work and they quit. Why should they work when they can get welfare?"

Liz: "I'm sure that there are some people on welfare who should be working, but just because you have come across one or two doesn't mean that they are all like that or that there are so many they make our taxes high."

Sally: "We do have a good cleaning lady who's one of them, but she says that everybody else where she lives is just living off welfare."

Liz: "Just how many is 'everybody'? You see two or three and you're angry because you work hard and they don't and you say 'everybody.' I'd like to know how many she means."

Sally: "Lots."

Tony: "There are plenty of jobs around. There's one station that broadcasts lists of jobs every week and you hear the same job week after week. You can say you've got to take care of poor people and, sure, you've got to if they're crippled or something. But most people if they're poor it's just because they're too lazy to work."

Liz: "Maybe they don't have enough education to get the jobs."

Tony: "What education do you need to clean up a shop or be a cleaning lady or a dishwasher? Anyway, if they don't have a good education it's their own fault. There are free schools for all, you know."

Frank: "Some people are on welfare and their parents were on welfare and their kids will be on welfare. It doesn't make sense, this whole system. Anybody can get on welfare and obviously nobody will work if he can get money without working."

Teacher: "Do you all agree with that?"

Voice from rear: "With what?"

Teacher: "That anybody can get on welfare and that no one will work if he can get income without doing any work."

Several: "Yes."

Teacher: "Then I'm going to ask you to raise your hands to show me something. Maybe I'm missing out on a good thing. I'm going to ask first to see the hands of those of you who are planning to take advantage of this system and go on welfare and—just a second—then to see the hands of those who are planning to work for a living or marry a man who will work for a living. Now, how many of you plan to go on welfare?"

(A few, "But that isn't . . ." but no hands.)

"How many plan to work?"

(Most hands up, but not all.)

"But you said anybody can go on welfare and that everybody would want to get the money without working for it. Are you different from everybody? Why are you planning to work? And what about you, Sue, you didn't choose either. Does welfare tempt you?"

Rick: "No, she's planning to marry a rich guy."

Teacher: "We'd better not get off on that. Why didn't the rest of you choose welfare?"

Frank: "Because we're not lazy the way they are and we're working hard enough in school to get jobs that pay a lot more than welfare."

Teacher: "I didn't realize that you were so ambitious and like to work so much. Let me give you a couple of extra reading assign . . ."

Rick: "We wouldn't want you to go to any trouble."

Teacher: "Back to the question, then. You are saying that there are enough jobs so that no one needs to be poor but that there are some people who are not hard working the way we are and are too lazy to take jobs and that it is these people who are on welfare?"

Liz: "Not just too lazy. We said that there were some who didn't have a good enough education."

Teacher: "I'm not sure that everyone agreed with that, Liz. Would you accept this? There are enough jobs and that there are opportunities for education for those who need it to take the jobs so no one needs to be poor, but some people are too lazy and so they're poor and on welfare."

Frank: "Yes."

Liz: "I don't . . ."

Sally: "Pretty much, yes. I mean, there are some people who are crippled or something and aren't lazy."

Teacher: "I think we all accept that."

Sally: "There ought to be a law saying that those who can work should or no welfare. I mean, if they refuse to work let them do without. They'll learn."

Teacher: "Isn't there such a law?"

Sally: "I don't know, but if there is they don't enforce it."

Teacher: "I was doing some work the other day *(Laughter)* and came across some figures quoted by one of the President's aides, Mr. Califano. They went like this." *(Writes on board.)*

    7.3   million people on welfare
    2.1   million are 65 or over

.7   million are blind or severely handicapped

3.5   million are children whose parents can't support them

.75   million are mothers of these children

.1   million are fathers of these children who are incapacitated

.05   million are people who could be self-supporting.

"Do these support the idea that the poor are poor just because they are lazy?"

Tony: "I bet a lot of those men who claim to be disabled are faking it. They could work if they wanted to and they would if it weren't for welfare."

Frank: "The important thing in those figures is the mothers and children. If those women go and have children when there's no husband around to take care of them that's their own fault. Why should we have to take care of them and their children just because they behave that way?"

Liz: "Would you make the children suffer just because the mothers aren't married?"

Frank: "There could be homes or something to take care of the kids and we could make the mothers work and pay the homes for taking care of them."

Tony: "Maybe we should add something to what you said before. Poor are poor because their morals are bad."

Liz: "Can we really judge whose morals are bad? Maybe it's their education."

Sally: "Well certainly . . ." *(Bell.)*

What Do You Think?

1.   This reading is entitled: "Why Should They Work When They Can Get Welfare?" How would you answer this question? Explain your reasoning.

2.   If there are some people who won't work because they can get welfare benefits equal to or greater than the amount they could earn, should this be ended by lowering welfare benefits or by raising wages? Explain.

3.   Was Frank correct in assuming that the man really owned the Buick? What is the basis for your opinion?

4.   Tony states: "Anyway, if they (the poor) don't have a good education it's their own fault. There are free schools for all, you know." How would you respond to this?

5.   To what extent can the poor be directly blamed for the poverty in which they live?

2.   PROMISES UNFULFILLED *

Poverty in some sections of the country can be explained in terms of the history and economic development of those areas. Certainly the poverty found on the Indian reservation described in Chapter 3 cannot be understood without remembering the things that were done to the Indian in earlier days. In the same way, as the following selection shows, what happened in Appalachia in the past affects that region today.

The poor of Appalachia are, in a very real sense, victims of history. This region, stretching from Georgia and Alabama in the south to Pennsylvania in the north and including large sections of West Virginia, Virginia, Kentucky, Tennessee, and North Carolina, has offered much but given little to its residents.

Appalachia has promised people a better way of life several times. These promises have lured people into the area and have kept them there.

The first promises were land, game, and freedom. Most of the early settlers were poorer people who had come to America from England, Scotland, and Ireland. Most had come voluntarily, but a few had been brought by force. As more and more of the tidewater lands were taken over by the large plantations, these poorer people moved to the west. There were game animals in the forests; there was land available in the valleys and coves (small recesses or areas between higher ground, very narrow where they start on the sides of the hills but becoming wider as they move down toward the broader valleys below); there was a chance to be independent. They settled in the valleys and moved up into the coves. As population increased they were forced farther up the coves until they reached areas where farming was nearly impossible. To meet the need for more land, they began to farm the hillsides. This led to erosion and new difficulties. It was possible to live on the game and on the produce of poor farms, but it was not possible to live well. Of the three promises, land, game, and freedom, only the last was really fulfilled. The mountaineer was independent and he has cherished his independence and individualism ever since.

The second great promise of prosperity came from the forests. When the settlers had arrived, the mountains had been covered with magnificent

---

* By David Durfee. See Harry Caudill, *Night Comes to the Cumberlands: A Biography of a Depressed Area*. Boston, Mass.: Little, Brown & Co. 1963, and Jack Weller, *Yesterday's People—Life in Contemporary Appalachia*. Louisville, Ky.: University of Kentucky Press, 1965.

trees, especially hardwoods such as oak and poplar. In the late Nineteenth Century speculators moved into the area offering what seemed fantastic sums to the mountaineers for the right to cut down and remove the trees from their land. In reality, the sums were nowhere near the true value of the timber. The mountaineer retained ownership of the land but the trees were the property of the speculator or the corporation to which he sold them. There was a wave of prosperity. In addition to the money he received for selling the timber rights, the mountaineer could earn wages performing dangerous logging operations. When the wave of prosperity ended, the mountains were barer and more eroded than before and the mountaineers were worse off than they had been before.

The last and greatest promise of prosperity was coal. The purchase of mineral rights reached its peak around the turn of the century. Mountaineers sold the rights for from $.50 to $5.00 an acre. A great industry and great fortunes were built on minerals that had once been the property of the mountaineers.

Coal mining brought destruction to much of the beauty of the region. Great mountains of discarded coal and slate grew. These frequently caught fire and remained burning slowly for years. Coal dust and smoke filled the air.

If ownership and beauty were gone, there were at least great employment opportunities. Prosperity was greatest during the period from World War I until the Depression. The population grew and it appeared that there would always be jobs for all. This was not to be, however. As the use of oil and gas and then atomic energy for fuel grew, the demand for coal declined. In order to compete with the producers of these other fuels, the coal companies replaced workers with machinery. Employment went way down and has stayed down ever since.

There are poor people in Appalachia today. People lured there by riches that no longer exist. People who no longer have either the treasures that the area had or the money they got for the sale of those treasures. Many of the younger people have moved out. The older folks have nothing to do but stay and get along somehow.

What Do You Think?

1. Is there any way in which the people of these mountains could have developed the riches themselves instead of selling them to outsiders? Where would they have gotten the capital needed to develop them?

2. Which do you think is the most important reason for the presence of poverty in Appalachia today, the kind of people who moved there in the first place, the out-of-the-way location of

Appalachia, or the way in which the timber and coal resources were exploited? Explain your reasoning.

3.   There are not enough jobs in Appalachia today. Would it be better to try to move new industries into the area or move the people who live there out? Explain.

3.   PROGRESS IS THE ENEMY *

Coal miners aren't the only people suffering unemployment because of the development of new machines. In a modern industrial state the pace of technological change is very rapid. Every day in both cities and rural areas men who have been trained to do a job are replaced by machines that can do the same job more rapidly and more economically. The situation is most tragic in the cases of those who are too old to learn a new skill or those who are capable only of unskilled labor in a land where it is no longer needed.

Cleosa Henley, whose hunger was described in Chapter 3, and others like him face this tragedy in the Black Belt.

Cleosa Henley and thousands of Negroes like him are the DP's [Displaced Persons] of a quiet revolution in the old cotton south. Once they were a fixed part of the landscape of the Black Belt, the fertile black crescent that runs thickest through Georgia, Alabama and Mississippi. But new cash crops (soybeans, wheat, timber, cattle) and a new cotton technology (mechanical pickers, chemical weed-killers) have made the old hoe hand expendable. The $1-an-hour minimum wage that went into effect for farm workers this year made him uneconomical. And the civil rights revolt, once it put the ballot in his hands, made him downright frightening to whites in areas with black majorities. Poor to begin with, the cottonfield Negro today is virtually obsolete—and poorer and hungrier than ever.

In this world, progress is often the enemy, and even the best intended government efforts to help sometimes become cruel jokes. Thus, the $1 minimum wage only spurred the Alabama Black Belt's interest in new crops. Greene County laid in its first 600 acres of soybeans in 1965, planted 17,000 acres [in 1967]—more than double the cotton acreage. "When we got rid of our niggers," says one planter, who has bulldozed most of his 200 tenant shacks, "we found out what money was." The wage law similarly sped up the delta's thrust into the technology of chemicals and machines. The tractor drivers stayed on, though

---

* From "Lord, I'm Hungry." Copyright *Newsweek,* Inc., July 24, 1967.

—with The Man keeping the books—$1 an hour tends to melt down to the same take home pay they got under the old rate of $6 a day. The real victims are the tenant wives and children and the "day haul" laborers who used to chop weeds in the spring and hand-pick cotton in the fall for $3 a day. The number of Negro pickers in the delta shrank, by one estimate, from 60,000 in 1959 to 2,000 [in 1966]—most of them working the edges of the fields where the machines miss a bit.

'ELIMINATIN''

But more than blind economic chance is at work. "Them white folks got a lot more interested in machinery after the civil rights bill was passed," one Black Belt Negro muses—and it is certainly true that the rights revolt has eroded Dixie's ancient paternalism. In the thickly wooded north end of Greene County, Alabama, "Miss Mary" Hixon, an ancient, feisty widow, still lives in her family's colonnaded ante-bellum mansion— and her thinned-out colony of tenants still occupies the old slave quarters out back. But Miss Mary has sold off much of her holdings to out-of-state buyers. "I wept bitterly when I sold the land," she says, "and all my nigras wept. But I couldn't keep 'em—they wouldn't work a lick. Ever since they got that civil rights bill they all figure the gov'ment will take care of them. I'll tell you one thing—if I was head of the Ku Klux, there'd be some eliminatin'."

"We thought if we lost our niggers, the world would come to an end," says another of the county's planters, Dave Johnston. But now he's recruiting white families in Missouri to work his 8,000 acres, much of it planted with soybeans, and he says: "The niggers is got to go. . . . It's like the deer. We got a lotta trouble with the deer eatin' our soybeans. We just wanta thin 'em out to where we can live with 'em."

What Do You Think?

1. Did the adoption of the civil rights voting act cause white owners to become more interested in machinery, or was it a coincidence that new crops like soybeans came in at the same time? What clues can you find in the reading?

2. Are minimum wage laws for farm workers likely to do such workers more harm or good in the long run?

3. What future would you predict for the "white families from Missouri" that were being recruited to work on the Johnston farm? Explain.

4.   NO ACCESS TO 'ACCESS' *

Poverty can be explained in terms of the failings of the poor them-selves. It can also be explained in terms of efforts of the well-to-do to protect their position by discriminating against the poor and espe-cially against the minority poor, as the following illustrates.

Many well meaning but misunderstanding whites look deep into the Negro ghettos of our larger cities, shudder at the sight and then say, "Why do they continue living there? Why don't they do like the Irish, the Italians, the Germans, and the Polish? Why don't they move into the mainstream, pull themselves up by their bootstraps, become an integral part of American society?"

These people are laboring under the same misapprehension that has kept most whites from a true understanding of the Negro's position in American history for years—the belief that Negroes have not, as other immigrants, taken advantage of the great rewards supposedly offered by American society to the able, the ambitious and the industrious.

LAND OF PROMISE

It is true that the United States, the last great "frontier" country, has been a land of promise to immigrants from nearly every nation in the world. Big, young, and rich in resources, the area which now comprises the United States can look back only 360 years to the establishment of the first English colony in Jamestown, Va., and can count only 191 years as an independent nation. In that short period of time as nations go, the U. S. has been first one of the world's leading agrarian nations and is now one of the most powerful in all history technologically. Science and technology have advanced so rapidly in this century that many persons born before the first successful flight of an airplane (the Wright Brothers, 1903) will still be alive to see television films of the first successful landing of a man on the moon.

Considering the tremendous progress of the United States as a whole, it is little wonder that one not familiar with the total history of the country could well ask, "Where has the Negro failed?"

IN FROM THE BEGINNING

To the uninitiated, the plight of the American Negro seems par-ticularly confusing when one considers that the Negro has been a part of

---

* An *Ebony* editorial by Herbert Nipson. Copyright © 1967, Johnson Publish-ing Co., Inc. Used by permission.

this country almost from the beginning. From 1619 until the present, the Negro has been a part of the population of what is now the U. S. From his humble slave beginning, he has grown in number, spread throughout the fifty states and has become a vast influence throughout the nation even though his affluence has lagged behind that of other "immigrants."

The United States is a nation of immigrants or descendants of immigrants. Of all the races and nations which people this country, only the misnamed "American Indian" (called Indian only because the early explorers thought that they had reached India instead of two vast, new continents—North and South America) is indigenous. Following—with two exceptions—the chronology of the waves of immigrants that peopled the U. S., a pecking order of prestige has grown up in this country. At the top is the white, Anglo-Saxon Protestant, descendant of the early colonists, the Daughters of the American Revolution type who too frequently feels that the nation would be much better off if everyone else had stayed home. Other Western Europeans (the Dutch, the German, the Scotch-Irish, French, Scandinavian, and Irish) follow in descending order. Then came the Mediterranean—particularly the Italian—followed by the Jewish, Slavic, Mexican and Latin American, Filipino, Middle Eastern, Oriental, and Puerto Rican.

The exceptions to the chronology are the American Indian, who was here to greet the explorers and colonists when they first arrived, and the Negro who was brought over in chains at about the same time the colonists debarked from their tiny ships. By chronology, they should rank at the top of the pecking order along with the Anglo-Saxon. Instead, they are at the bottom and it is a tossup as to which is in the absolute basement.

NO ACCESS TO 'ACCESS'

The brilliant editor, educator, and author Max Lerner, himself an immigrant who came to the U. S. as a child with his parents from Minsk, Russia, in 1907, was once asked to summarize in a single word the keystone of American development. He answered: "Access. By this I mean access to economic opportunity, access to social mobility, access to geographic movement, access to political participation. Most important of all, perhaps, would be access to educational opportunity."

Dr. Lerner's succinct summing up of the reason America and Americans could advance so readily need only be negatized to give the answers to the questions asked by the well-meaning whites in the first paragraph of this editorial. The American Negro is in the position he is in today because access to practically everything Lerner has mentioned has been denied him while it has remained open to almost every other immigrant who has come to these shores. For his first 244 years in the U. S. the Negro not only had no access to economic opportunity but lived primarily as a slave in a slave economy that made him an economic product to be bought and sold by slave owners. After the Emancipation Proclamation, the Negro found himself free in name only. Trained to work in a slave economy, he found himself the last hired and first fired for more than a century. Performing the hard hand labor, the domestic work, the jobs that no one else wanted, he was lucky to keep food in his children's mouths and a roof over his head. He had no access to the free land available for settlement in the West; he had no access to the gold rushes, the timberland steals, the establishment of new businesses, the free grazing land, the oil explorations, etc. which brought riches to many whites.

NO SOCIAL MOBILITY

Dr. Lerner's social mobility was and, with rare exceptions, still is a myth so far as the American Negro is concerned. Even so august a person as the UN's Ralph Bunche found, when he tried to join a tennis club in New York, that a Negro cannot escape his race. Under American society as it is structured today, the Negro has developed a society within a society. A Negro can rise from the slums to middle class, even to wealth within the Negro society and yet have no more status than the slum dweller when the American society as a whole is taken into consideration.

That the Negro has had no true access to full political participation can be proved by the fact that so few Negroes hold statewide offices and by the fact that federal registrars must be sent to many parts of the South just to assure a Negro his right to cast a vote.

Access to educational opportunity is still not something a Negro can take for granted. The children of Grenada, Miss., found themselves brutally beaten by white adults merely because they were attempting to exercise their legal right to attend an integrated elementary school. Until recent years, many colleges and universities in the North discouraged Negro attendance by not granting Negroes room in dormitories and dining halls. And even today, the Negro ghetto elementary and secondary schools of Northern cities are grossly inferior.

THE RIGHT TO TRAVEL

The one access mentioned by Dr. Lerner that has been open to Negroes is the access to geographic movement. He has really taken advantage of this access. The Negro left the South literally by the millions, traveling north and west. He spread himself throughout the urban centers of the entire country. The only trouble was, once he got where he was going he found the other accesses closed to him.

So the next time misunderstanding whites ask, "Why don't they move into the mainstream?" tell them. Tell them to help us open the doors.

---

1. Is there a relationship between discrimination and poverty? Is it as direct as this article indicates? Explain your answer.
2. Is there really a "pecking order" in America based on the sequence in which different national groups arrived?
3. Mr. Nipson speaks rather sarcastically of a "Daughters of the American Revolution type." What does he mean by this? How might a member of the D.A.R. respond to this? Explain.
4. If you were to list all of the people you actually know in the order of their social position (where they stand in the "pecking order"), how far up the list would the highest Black be? How would you explain this?

5. MISPLACED EMPHASES IN WARS ON POVERTY *

The first two articles in this chapter presented views placing the blame for poverty on bigotry or laziness. Some experts, however, feel that mistakes made by people with good intentions are at least as important as deliberate actions taken by middle-class whites or lazy welfare recipients.

Simon Rottenberg, Professor of Economics at Duke University, has listed some of the government programs which he believes have helped to produce poverty rather than to lessen it. Portions of his list follow.

An examination of various facets of public policy in the United States will show that some fraction of poverty which we encounter among the people is, in fact, produced by government. Those who promote these policies do not, of course, intend nor desire that they shall have these effects; indeed, some of them are thought to promote progress and ameliorate poverty. Their enactment and execution is a tribute to the power in the world of the naïve cliché. Only some of these poverty-producing policies will be discussed.

---

* Reprinted with permission from a symposium, *Anti-poverty Programs,* appearing in *Law and Contemporary Problems* (Vol. 31, No. 1, Winter 1966) published by the Duke University School of Law, Durham, North Carolina. Copyright, 1966, by Duke University.

1. The Fair Labor Standards Act of 1938 establishes a legal minimum hourly wage for those employed in a large sector of the economy. This minimum is probably irrelevant for most workers who, even in the absence of the law, would be paid more than the law requires. It is not irrelevant, however, for those in the lowest-skill classes. The law requires that wages paid in some unskilled occupations be higher than the level at which the market would set them. The consequence is that a smaller number of workers is employed in those occupations than would be if there were no minimum wage law, because firms seeking lowest-cost resource combinations are given an incentive to use substitutes for now more expensive unskilled labor. Workers who would have been employed in those occupations but who are kept from them by the law's higher wage standards are either forced into unemployment or enter occupations that are not covered by the law. In these occupations they are worse off than they would have been. . . .

2. The National Labor Relations Act establishes procedures to determine whether workers in a "bargaining unit" desire to be represented by a trade union and, if their decision is affirmative, requires that firms negotiate with the relevant union the terms of employment. The act promotes trade unionism. If a union is effective (*i.e.,* if it is not innocuous), the rate of wages in the occupations to which it has reference will be higher than the rate that would have prevailed in the absence of unionism. . . . Such a higher wage rate has the same adverse employment consequences and the same depressant effects upon wages paid in other occupations as do minimum wage laws. Some workers (those who *are* employed at the higher rates) are privileged at the cost of other workers. . . .

3. Farming in the United States is a declining occupation, measured by the relative numbers of persons employed in it. The outmigration from farming is responsive to superior earnings in other sectors, and the relatively low earnings in agriculture can be taken as a proxy for relatively low productivity of employment in agriculture. Output for the economy as a whole would be larger if fewer persons were employed in agriculture and more in other sectors. At least since the middle of the 1930's, public policy has subsidized farmers at the expense of the rest of the community and this has had the effect of diminishing the rate of outmigration from agriculture. Whatever induces people to remain in agriculture will have adverse output consequences and, thus, will tend to enlarge the quantity of poverty.

4. The Social Security Act requires most employed persons to purchase an annuity which is paid to them after they have reached a qualifying age but only if they substantially retire from employment. The annuity is withheld from those older persons who continue to work. The specific form of the rule is that the annuity will not be paid to those whose earn-

ings from employment exceed a specified number of dollars in a year. . . . Some older persons who would be otherwise disposed to continue to work are induced by the law to stop. If they do not stop, they may not have their annuity benefit. The output of the whole economy is, therefore, less by some magnitude; the smaller the output, the larger the quantity of poverty. And the policy precisely induces older people to earn less. The act generates poverty among the aged.

*   *   *   *   *

7. A policy of equal-pay-for-equal-work for men and women is common among the states. Such a policy makes it less attractive for firms to employ women rather than men. It is a policy that favors men over women by assuring men that women will offer them less competition for employment and that damages women by driving them to unemployment or to second-best employment options. Women who are heads of families are made worse off by it.

8. The incidence of poverty rises with rising numbers of children in the family. Whatever encourages parents to produce more offspring will produce more poverty. While the magnitude of the effect may not be large, the policy of granting exemption from income tax for children when computing tax liability will tend in that direction.

9. The amount of poverty in a community is a function of the quantity of goods and services it produces in some time period and of the distribution of income. Given the distribution, the more that is produced the less poverty there will be. . . . Some welfare payments to the poor and some unemployment benefits, by providing substitute "earnings" for those that would be yielded by work, diminish incentives to work and cause output to be smaller. . . . Unemployment benefits received under some insurance systems are especially vulnerable in this respect since the failure to work is precisely a condition for their payment.

What Do You Think?

1. Would poverty be lessened if these various laws were repealed? Explain your answer. Consider each argument. What points would you offer in rebuttal?

2. Would you agree with the statement, "Given the distribution, the more that is produced the less poverty there will be"?

3. Professor Rottenberg argues that women are hurt by the law requiring that they be given equal pay for equal work. Would most women oppose or support this law? How can this be explained?

6.   FACES OF THE POOR *

Poverty can also be understood in individual terms. The physical and mental characteristics which a person inherits may limit his ability to compete successfully in a modern urban society. Other individuals who are born without any such limitations may be reduced to poverty because of some accident or misfortune that overtakes them. Still others may find themselves poor just because they have grown too old to work. This last situation was seen in the article "Old People Have to Eat Well to Keep Out of the Hospital," in Chapter 3. The sketches which follow illustrate biological limitations and misfortunes.

Francis

Francis appeared to be perfectly normal at birth. His parents were delighted by his arrival for they had wanted a child for some years. The father was a bus maintenance man working in the garage of the local transit company. His income was adequate but there was not much left over after regular living costs had been paid. The mother had encountered a series of illnesses which had both used up all of the family cash reserves and prevented them from having children earlier. When Francis was born, his father was 39 and his mother 36.

As an only child, he was the object of a great amount of attention at home. His parents tried to be with him as much as possible and to anticipate his every desire. When Francis was slow in standing up and in developing the ability to manipulate his toys, neighbors told his parents that it was because they did everything for the boy. In any case, he was not far behind the average child. The parents did worry, however, for they had ambitious plans for the boy. He was certainly to go to college and then into business or perhaps even into a profession. They wanted him to have all of the advantages that they had not had.

At five Francis entered kindergarten and then went on to first grade. His progress was reported as "normal" for the first three years of schooling, however teachers complained that he was very slow in following directions that were given to the class. In third grade he started dropping behind, especially in reading. His parents became quite upset, and Francis was aware of this. He became more and more disruptive in school. The mother and father talked about withdrawing him from public school and

---

* Based upon composite cases. See similar sketches in "The Hundred Neediest Cases," *The New York Times,* each December, and Arthur Simon, *Faces of Poverty.* St. Louis, Mo.: Concordia Publishing House, 1966.

sending him to a private one where he would receive special attention, but continued illness by the mother made this financially impossible. The situation at home became more and more tense, and his relations with both teachers and students at school continued to deteriorate.

Tests given at the school revealed two things. The first was that his hearing was somewhat below normal, a condition which had apparently existed since birth and probably explained his slowness in following instructions. The second was that his I.Q. tested out to about 87. It became clear to the parents that their great ambitions for him would never be realized.

Francis failed to pass sixth grade and had to repeat the year. When the class was divided into groups based on ability in the eighth grade, he was placed in the slowest track. When he failed English, social studies, and math in tenth grade and it became obvious that he would lose another year, he gained his parents' reluctant consent to quit school.

After two years of part-time yard work and other odd jobs he moved out of his parents' apartment, which he now found intolerable. For a short period of time he found steady employment at $1.40 an hour with a gas company crew laying down new pipelines. The work was hard and there was no chance for advancement, given his educational background and limited intelligence. Living alone proved to be expensive, and he quit the job hoping to find something better.

Since that time he has had a few temporary jobs, has had three brushes with the law, although not serious, and has become more and more discouraged. His home is now a bug-infested rooming house in a slum area.

Louise

Unlike Francis, Louise was a completely normal child. Her I.Q. was 110 and her hearing and sight were all that they should be. In school she was in the upper third of her class. She was attractive and energetic. Life looked very promising—until she was 13. There was an automobile accident. Her mother was killed, her father was crippled, and she was very seriously hurt. The doctors did all that they could but could not erase the scars on the left side of her face, and they found it necessary to replace her left eye with a glass one.

While the insurance money lasted, a housekeeper took care of the father, and Louise returned to school. It was different now, however. Most people tried to be kind, but she could sense a feeling of revulsion.

When she turned sixteen, Louise left school. This was partly because of the behavior of the students and partly because her father's money had just about given out and she was needed at home to care for him. Since that time she has thought occasionally of taking night secretarial courses but fears that it would be useless because no one would want her in an office anyway.

The money is gone now and they have applied for welfare assistance.

What Do You Think?

1.   Are there any other things besides the limited I.Q. and hearing with which Francis was born that might explain his current poverty? Could he have overcome these handicaps? Could you have?

2.   Did the school do all that it could to meet Francis' needs? Explain your answer.

3.   Would it have made any difference in Louise's case if her parents had been very wealthy before the accident?

ACTIVITIES FOR INVOLVEMENT

1.   Make a study of the want ads in your local paper over a period of a week or more. Determine and report to the class on:

a.   How many ads there are for jobs which do not require special skills.

b.   How many of the ads for unskilled labor appear day after day. Is this evidence that there are jobs that no one is willing to take?

c.   How many of the unskilled jobs are seasonal ones and how many appear to be permanent?

2.   Select an area of the country other than Appalachia in which there is a great amount of poverty. Do some research into the history of that area and write an explanation of the historical reasons for poverty there.

3.   Select one of the areas of "access" discussed in the article "No Access to 'Access'." Using materials on American history as sources, write a description of the methods that have been used to deny this particular access to Negroes. Is there more access in this area now than there has been in the past?

4.   Do some research into automation. List the arguments that indicate that technological progress will provide more jobs and those that indicate that it will destroy more jobs than it creates. Which set of arguments is more convincing? Why?

5.   Write an editorial responding to Professor Rottenberg's article. How would you support one of the laws that he criticizes?

6.   Professor Rottenberg says, "Given the distribution, the more that is produced the less poverty there will be." Find out what the current gross national product is. What increase in the gross national product would be needed to raise the income of a family from $2,000 a year to $4,000 a year if distribution remained the same?

How Much Poverty Exists in America?

5

The election campaign of 1960 which raised the issue of poverty took place during a census year. Figures from the 1960 census were used in efforts to determine just how many poor people there were in America. Families with incomes below $3,000 per year and unattached individuals with incomes below $1500 were classified as "poor." On the basis of the 1960 census figures the number of people in the United States living below these income levels was put at almost 35,000,000. This was nearly one-fifth of the total population!

As inflation has continued since that time the minimum income needed to escape from the poverty classification has gone up. By 1967, for example, the family figure most frequently cited was $3,300 and the individual figure was $1,650.

The $3,000 and $1,500 figures used in interpreting the 1960 census were derived from a study made by the U. S. Department of Labor in 1959 concerning the amount of income needed for an adequate standard of living in the United States. Though the amount needed varied from place to place, it averaged about $6,000 for a family of four.

The $3,000 figure was chosen, therefore, because it was just half of the amount which people needed to maintain an adequate standard of living. Census readers described those families and individuals with incomes between the poverty line and the "adequate" line as "deprived." The deprived numbered about 30,000,000 in 1960. Adding the number of deprived to the number of those living in poverty gave a figure of 65,000,000. This figure represented over one-third of the population in 1960.

These estimates did not go without challenge. Other men studied the same census figures and their meaning and reported that they certainly did not prove that there were so many millions of Americans living in poverty or deprivation. They insisted that low dollar income did not necessarily mean a low standard of living or hopeless poverty but that each case had to be evaluated separately. They also argued that most of those with incomes under $3,000 seemed to enjoy many of the better things in life normally considered to be luxury items.

These two views of the extent of poverty are obviously in conflict with each other. Just how much poverty and destitution does exist in America? The readings which follow should help you decide.

1. THE EXTENT OF POVERTY IN THE U. S. *

Among the groups most concerned about the extent of poverty is the Conference of Economic Progress headed by Leon H. Keyserling, who was the chairman of President Truman's Council of Economic Advisers. The following excerpts are taken from his findings.

POVERTY MEANS TOO LITTLE INCOME

Descriptions of the poor by color or race, age or sex, geographic location, type of employment or lack of job opportunity should never distract us from *the one universal characteristic of all the poor:* they do not receive enough income in money and other forms to rise above poverty. Only programs which increase their incomes can reduce poverty.

Although the poor also need public services (such as education) which they do not pay for directly out of their personal incomes (but pay for through taxes which frequently hit them all too regressively at the local level), personal income received is by far the best practical *measurement* of whether people are poor. Undoubtedly, most of those regarded as poor in the U. S. today have a level of consumption incomparably higher than many not considered poor in India today; they may live better in some respects than many not considered poor in the U. S. fifty years ago—and even enjoy some products which rich families could not get fifty years ago. Thus, the very concept of poverty must attach some weight to the stage of our technology, wealth, and capabilities.

But this does not make the concept of poverty merely a *relative* matter. For example, when we say that almost one-fifth of the people in the U. S. are poor today, we do not mean that the lowest fifth should *always* be regarded as poor. If the lowest fifth a generation hence should

---

* Excerpted from Leon H. Keyserling, *Progress or Poverty: The U. S. at the Crossroads.* Washington, D. C.: Conference on Economic Progress, 1964.

come to enjoy average family incomes of $10,000 a year measured in 1964 dollars, we would not say that all of these people were still poor because they were still in the lowest income fifth. The observation that almost a fifth of our people are poor today means simply this: their incomes now are very far below the levels required to enable them to enjoy minimum *objective* standards which knowledgeable people deem to be even barely adequate on the current American scene, with respect to food, clothing, housing, medical care, education, rewarding leisure, and a reasonable margin of savings beyond what they spend.

HOW MUCH POVERTY DO WE HAVE NOW?

In 1963, the number of families living in poverty with incomes under $3,000 . . . was 8.9 million or an estimated 29.2 million people. The number of unattached individuals living in poverty, with incomes under $1,500, was 5 million. The total number of people living in poverty thus came to 34.2 million, or between a fifth and sixth of a nation.

More tragically still, in 1963 the number of families with incomes under $2,000 was 5.1 million, or 16.7 million people. And the number of unattached individuals with incomes under $1,000 was 3.2 million. Thus, almost 20 million people, or substantially more than a tenth of a nation, were at least 33⅓ per cent *below* the income levels needed to lift them out of the poverty cellar.

And none of the data just cited convey the full meaning of poverty. For the *average* income of all families under $3,000 in 1963 was only $1,778; the *average* for all families "under $2,000" was only $1,220; the *average* for the 1.8 million families "under $1,000" was only $630.

THE AMOUNT OF PROGRESS OVER THE YEARS

During the sixteen years from 1947 to 1963, the number of families living in poverty was reduced from 12 million to 8.9 million. The average annual reduction was less than 0.2 million families, or only about 1.9 per cent a year. If the same percentage rate should continue in the future, it would take another 45 years to liquidate family poverty in the United States. Such delay is unacceptable.

EXTENT OF DEPRIVATION IN THE U.S.

We have already noted that the *average* income requirement for a "modest but adequate" budget is in the neighborhood of *$6,000* for a family, and about *$2,750* for an unattached individual. Thus it appears conservatively that families with incomes below *$5,000* but above the poverty level, and unattached individuals with incomes below *$2,500* but above the poverty level, are living in deprivation, especially as the *average* income of these people falls far *below* $5,000 and $2,250, respectively.

In 1963, 8.6 million American families, an estimated 30 million people, and 1.9 million unattached individuals, lived in deprivation: a total of about 32 million, or more than a sixth of a nation. Adding those living in poverty, more than 66 million people, or about 35½ per cent of our population, lived either in poverty or deprivation in 1963.

Those living in deprivation are denied that participation in the wealth and well-being of our economic society which they should enjoy. Even though not "poor," they at no time experience an American standard of living, and a majority of them are threatened with poverty in the event of any adverse turn. Moreover, the many millions who are deprived live under special psychological, social, and moral pressures. Their lot is ironic: the vast majority of them have breadwinners who are hard-working and employed, and thus they have obtained "respectability"; but their right to a respectable level of living has not been honored.

What Do You Think?

1. Keyserling says that if the pace at which poverty is being eliminated continues to be the same, it will take 45 years from 1963 (40 years from 1968 or 35 years from 1973) to eliminate poverty and that such a delay is unacceptable. Would you agree? Explain.

2. The figures indicate that more than one American out of every three lives in poverty or deprivation. Do your own experiences and observations confirm this? What possible explanations are there if they do not?

3. Keyserling says that one-fifth of all Americans do not enjoy the minimum objective standards deemed adequate on the current American scene. Are human needs objective or are they relative? Do we "need" more things than our grandparents did?

4. One "need" that is listed is savings. Are savings a necessity or a luxury in modern America? Explain your reasoning.

2. IS THE U. S. REALLY FILLED WITH POVERTY? *

Some experts are very critical of figures that show from 35 to 75 million poor and deprived people in America. They argue that you can-

---

* By John B. Parrish, Professor of Economics, University of Illinois. Reprinted from *U. S. News & World Report.* Copyright 1967 U. S. News & World Report, Inc.

not determine whether or not a person lives in poverty just by looking at how much money he makes. The following article, for example, suggests that if the way in which people with low incomes live is examined, it will prove that the number of poor and deprived people in America has been grossly exaggerated.

When future historians write the history of the 1960's, there will be no more extraordinary episode in their accounts than the rise of America's "new poverty" cult. Intellectuals from every social-science discipline, every religious denomination, every political and social institution have climbed aboard the poverty bandwagon.

This article is concerned with a few fundamental questions: How did the new cult get started? What are its claims? Does the economic evidence support the claims? Are we moving toward a new and better social order or toward social chaos?

After a decade of exploring every nook and cranny of the poverty world, the "new poverty" cult has settled on a few basic doctrines which together form a dogma that apparently must be accepted on faith. These claims may be briefly summarized as follows:

1. The economic process, which in earlier years brought affluence to a majority of Americans, recently has slowed up and apparently stopped. As a result, a large minority of Americans are "hopelessly" trapped below the poverty line.
2. The size of this poverty population is "massive," and may be increasing. Minimum estimates place the number at 30 million, maximum at nearly 80 million.
3. Despite its great size, the poverty population is hidden away— "invisible," unknown, unwanted, unaided, helpless.
4. The hard core of the "other America" is the Negro. Because of racial discrimination, he has been unable to participate in economic progress. He is frustrated, embittered, forced to live outside the affluent society of the majority.
5. The "new poverty" can only be eradicated by massive, federal social-action programs involving income maintenance, self-help, education and training, in a milieu of racial integration, the latter voluntary if possible, compulsory if necessary.

Does the evidence on diffusion of economic well-being support the "new poverty" cult? Has diffusion mysteriously slowed to a halt leaving millions "hopelessly trapped"? Are 30 to 80 million suffering acute deprivation in today's America? The plain truth is there is no basis in fact for the "new poverty" thesis. The high priests of the poverty religion have been exchanging each other's misinformation. Let's look briefly at some illustrative evidence.

DIET

The diet of U. S. families has continued to improve steadily over time until today at least 95 per cent, perhaps 96 per cent or 97 per cent of all families have an adequate minimum daily intake of nutrients.

AUTOMATIC COOKING EQUIPMENT

Are 20 per cent, perhaps 40 per cent, of U. S. families without decent equipment with which to prepare this food intake? No. As a matter of fact, 99 per cent of all U. S. households have automatic cooking equipment, including most of those families living in rural and urban "ghettos." The diffusion has been consistent and persistent over the last six decades.

REFRIGERATION

Could it be that millions of American families are experiencing dull and dreary meals because they have no way to preserve foods and beverages against spoilage? No. About 99 per cent of all U. S. families have purchased electric or gas refrigerators. It is reasonable to assume they know how to operate them, even in the "ghettos."

COMMUNICATION

Are millions of America's poor shut off from all contact with the rest of their affluent countrymen—alone, frustrated, in that "other world" of poverty isolation? At last count, the diffusion of TV sets had reached 92 per cent of all U. S. households, providing instant access to entertainment, news, sports, cultural enrichment. Since a small per cent of middle and upper income families who can afford TV have chosen not to buy, the per cent of families having TV who want it must be around 96 or 97 per cent—a diffusion achieved in just 15 years.

MEDICAL AID

Have the "new helpless poor" found the doors to modern medical service "slammed shut," forcing them to rely on quack remedies, superstition, midwives, or to die alone and unattended?

In 1910 only one in every 10 American families had access to hospitals for childbirth. The diffusion since then has been spectacular and persistent for all groups, including nonwhites. By 1960, over 97 per cent of all American women had their babies born in hospitals. Today it is somewhere between 98 per cent and 99 per cent.

THE LUXURY OF TELEPHONE SERVICE

Telephone service is ordinarily not a rock-bottom consumer necessity. It is useful and convenient but not an absolute requirement, as was demonstrated during the Great Depression of the 1930's when the per cent of families with telephones declined.

Yet today nearly 90 per cent of all U. S. households have telephones. Since there are still a few pockets of unavailability, it is reasonable to conclude that close to 95 per cent of all U. S. households in availability areas who would like this luxury actually enjoy it.

"Three Poverty Fallacies"

The foregoing illustrative evidence raises an interesting question: *How can the "massive" group of America's "hopeless poor" buy so much with so little?* Perhaps this basic question can be put another way: How could the poverty intellectuals be so wrong? The answer is actually very simple. The intellectuals have chosen to be wrong. Most members of the "new poverty" cult are quite well-trained in statistics. Some are acknowledged experts. They know better. But, for the sake of the "new poverty" religion, they have chosen to accept three poverty fallacies.

The "new poverty" cult has built much of its case on family-income statistics. Some technical matters aside, there is nothing wrong with these statistics, per se. But there is something wrong, very much wrong, with their use. It is impossible for anyone adequately to interpret them in terms of average family economic well-being.

Poverty fallacy No. 1 got its big push from the 1964 report on "The Problem of Poverty in America" by the Council of Economic Advisers. CEA determined that households with less than $3,000 annual income were in poverty. Using this income yardstick, it was determined that 20 per cent of U. S. households containing 30 million persons were in the poverty class.

This report provided a wonderful takeoff point for poverty statisticians. With 30 million to build on, it was not difficult to find millions of additional families who should be added to the poverty population. The poverty numbers game became quite exciting. Who could count the most? Honors so far have gone to those claiming nearly 80 million. A majority of cult members have settled for a more modest 40 to 50 million.

The truth about poverty-income statistics is this: Under no reasonable assumptions does any income below $3,000 indicate poverty status. It may or may not, and to say otherwise is not only erroneous but absurd.

Let's take as an example a young married couple, the Smiths. They are attending college. They constitute a statistical household. Their annual income is $1,500 a year. They are not being "hopelessly" shut out from the good things of life. They are, along with other American youth, enjoying a rate of access to higher education greater than the youth of any country, any time, any place. They enjoy electric lighting, refrigeration, adequate if not fancy food, and a second-hand automobile or motorcycle. They would like a new Cadillac, but will manage without one. They aren't "poor" and need no crocodile tears shed in their behalf.

At the other end of the life cycle are the Joneses. Mr. Jones has been a machinist all his life. He and Mrs. Jones had always wanted to visit the country's great national parks after the children had grown up and left. So he has opted to retire at age 60. The retirement income will come to only $2,000 a year. Are they poor? The poverty cult says, "Yes," these people are suffering from deprivation. They have been "hopelessly" cast aside. Yet the truth is they have a small home paid for, a modest automobile paid for. They enjoy refrigeration, automatic cooking equipment, inside plumbing, TV, enough clothes to last for years—the accumulation of a lifetime. And now they propose to enjoy more leisure, in more comfort, for more years than similar working-class families of any country, any time. The Joneses think the Council of Economic Advisers is statistically wacky.

And take the Browns. They are in the middle years. Both Mr. and Mrs. Brown work. Their three children are in school. They have a modest new home, partially paid for, some savings, some insurance, good clothes —yes, and a paid-for refrigerator and TV set. They have a new car and six installments still outstanding. Mr. Brown becomes ill. Mrs. Brown quits work to take care of him. Their income drops to below $3,000 for the year. Are they in trouble? Yes. Are they in desperate consumer poverty? Are they "hopelessly trapped"? By no means. After a tough year they will resume as members of the affluent society even by CEA's definition.

Economic Well-Being: "Cumulative"

These illustrations could be multiplied many times. Cross-section household-income statistics are a very inappropriate yardstick with which to measure economic well-being, which is a longitudinal and cumulative process.

Let's return for a moment to the telephone as a luxury—or at least a semiluxury—consumer good. Now take the desperately poor on whom the doors of affluency have presumably been "slammed shut." Now take the "poorest of the poor"—those at the very rock bottom of the income scale, those desperately deprived households earning less than $500 a year. You just can't get much poorer than that.

Now observe that nearly 60 per cent of these poorest of the poor had telephone service in 1965. How could this be? Why would families presumably facing the grim miseries of malnutrition order telephone service? And, if we make allowance for the availability factor and the "can afford but don't want" factor, then it is reasonable to conclude that 70 to 80 per cent of America's poorest poor had telephones in 1965.

If this is the "new poverty," it is apparently not too severe. How to explain this paradox of income poverty, consumer-goods affluence?

The answer is quite simple. Income data are a very bad measure of economic well-being. The Smiths, the Joneses, the Browns, all had telephone service even though the CEA's income statistics put them in the "poverty class."

There is a second big fallacy in the "new poverty" claims, and in some respects an inexcusable one. The poverty cult measures the economic well-being of families at all income levels by determining what they can buy with their income at current retail prices. In fact, the poverty cult makes much out of the fact that because of the greed of retail merchants and the gullibility and lack of buying savvy on the part of many poor buyers, the "new poor" actually pay more for the same goods than the affluent classes. This is hogwash.

The truth is, America's low-income classes have access to a low-price consumer-goods market in which prices are a fraction of published retail prices, and in which the purchasing power of "poor" dollars is multiplied many times. This discount market yields levels of consumption far above that indicated by retail prices.

As the poor could explain to CEA and the poverty intellectuals, this market is America's enormously big resale market—the world's largest. Every year, from 25 to 65 per cent of many consumer durable-goods purchases involve second- or third-hand goods moving in established trade or in informal person-to-person channels.

Take as an example a popular consumer durable good, the electric refrigerator. In 1923, this appliance was a new item. In current dollars, it cost around $900. Its capacity was small, averaging less than 6 cubic feet. It averaged only six years of service life, or about $150 a year. There were too few produced, and service was too short for a resale market. Only the rich could afford a refrigerator.

Today a good new refrigerator can be purchased for about $300. Its capacity will average about 10 cubic feet. Service life will be around 18 years. The average replacement year currently is around 10. So the first buyer pays about $30 a year, minus trade-in. Resale value will be about $50. This will permit the second buyer to purchase eight years of the same quality of refrigeration for about $6 a year. The low-income buyer, not particular about the latest style, has expanded his purchasing power 500 per cent over that of the first high-income buyer.

Today's low-income, "new poverty" buyer has purchasing power 25 times greater than that of the rich buyer of 1923. America's consumer durable-goods market is operating under a law of accelerating diffusion. America's low-income families are not being shut out. They are being pulled into affluence at an ever-increasing rate.

There is a big, hidden, tertiary consumer-goods market not measured even by retail or resale price statistics. This is the intergeneration movement of goods accumulated over time and handed down or distributed from one generation to another. In an affluent society this becomes a very large market. Sewing machines, automobiles, electric irons, kitchenware, furniture, silverware, dinnerware, bicycles, etc.—all these provide an enormous source of consumption for all income classes, including the poor.

Growth of No-Cost Goods, Services

If ignoring the durable-goods resale market is inexcusable, the failure of the poverty cult to take account of the rapid growth in low-cost or no-cost goods and services in America is well-nigh incredible. It is incredible because much of it has been brought about by the very federal agencies whose economists have been among the high priests of the poverty cult. This failure constitutes poverty fallacy No. 3.

To illustrate: Nearly 90 per cent of all Negro births today are in hospitals. Yet the U. S. House Committee on Education and Labor in 1964 said half the Negroes in America were suffering from acute poverty, measured by income statistics. How can so many poor afford so much medical service? For two reasons: First, as already noted, the income data are faulty. But more to the point here, almost every urban community has free or very low-cost medical services for low-income families. In fact, surveys show that in some communities the lowest-income families have more medical checkups, vaccinations, chest X-rays, eye examinations than some higher income groups.

The number of low-cost food programs has been growing rapidly. For example, the national school-lunch program provided low-cost noon meals for nearly 20 million children in 1967. The food-stamp plan provided low-cost food for 1 million persons in 1966, and was scheduled to rise to 2 million in 1967. The low-cost milk plan, along with school lunch, accounted for 5 per cent of total U. S. nonfarm fluid-milk consumption in 1966, and would have expanded even more in 1967 had not cutbacks been ordered because of Vietnam.

The total number of low-income persons reached by various food-subsidy programs came to nearly 30 million in 1966, or precisely the number of persons classified as poor in 1964 by the Council of Economic Advisers. Since many of the CEA's 30 million didn't belong in the poverty classification in the first place, some questions may well be raised as to who and how many poor have been "forgotten."

What Do You Think?

1. Is possession of or lack of consumer durable-goods such as refrigerators, washing machines, and television sets a better

standard for determining poverty or affluence than family income? Why or why not?

2.   A study made in 1968 indicated that 10,000,000 Americans suffered from hunger and malnutrition. How do these figures compare with those given by the author of this article? How can you explain the differences in the way in which they are stated?

3.   The author states that many who have claimed much higher numbers of poor than he believes exist "know better" than some of the claims they make and that they are guilty of inexcusable fallacies. Would anyone want to find more poverty than actually existed? Explain. Would anyone want to find less? Explain.

4.   There are three descriptions of families with low incomes in the article. Do you agree with the author that none of these should be classed as living in poverty? Explain.

ACTIVITIES FOR INVOLVEMENT

1.   Reread the selections in Chapter 3, all of which describe specific situations. As you read note all evidence of the amount of income and of whether or not the people enjoy the goods and services described by Parrish. Use the evidence thus gained in writing a paper supporting either Keyserling or Parrish.

2.   Keyserling reports that of the 34 million Americans with incomes under the poverty level:

52 per cent reflect deficient education
44 per cent live in the South
40 per cent reflect excessive unemployment
29 per cent reflect female family heads
27 per cent reflect aged family heads
25 per cent are nonwhite
15 per cent live on farms

Arrange these categories in the order of the "hopelessness" of the condition. Be prepared to defend your arrangement. Compare your listing with those of your classmates. What differences do you notice? Similarities? How would you explain these differences and similarities?

3.   Write a description similar in style to those of the Smiths, Joneses, and Browns in the second article in this chapter. Try to describe families and individuals as close to the poverty line as possible, with some just above it and some just below. Share your descriptions with the rest of the class. Do all members of the class agree as to which cases are really poverty cases? Hold a class discussion in which you try to establish standards that can be used to determine whether or not a person lives in poverty.

4.   The author of the second article in this chapter lists five basic "doctrines" which, he believes, form the dogma of the members of the poverty cult. Review the work of one of these people (Keyserling or Har-

rington or one of those listed in the bibliography at the back of the book) and report on how many of these doctrines you have found in it. Would you support any of these doctrines you have found? Why or why not?

5.   Statistics can be used in different ways and so can words. Go through the two articles in this chapter and list the words that are used for their emotional effect rather than the objective information which they convey.

6.   Make a list of several consumer items that have been available for varying amounts of time (for example, 50 years, 20 years, five years, and six months). Conduct a poll, without requiring those who respond to give their names, to find which items people have in their home. What conclusions can you draw about diffusion? Do these conclusions support or contradict the statements made in the second article in this chapter on this subject? Explain.

What Are the Effects of Poverty?

The economic effects of poverty on the poor themselves are obvious.

It is easy to see and to understand the economic effects that poverty has on the poor themselves. They must put up with an inadequate diet, with substandard housing, with doing without the goods and services that everyone else seems to enjoy in the affluent society.

Are there other effects, however, that may be less visible but just as serious—effects that hurt not only the poor but all other members of the society and which may even endanger the country? What, for example, is the effect of poverty on respect for law? On family life? On education? On loyalty to country? If poverty weakens these, then it does more than economic harm. The first four readings in this chapter should help you to draw some conclusions about these questions. Is poverty a major cause of the riots that have swept America since 1963? If so, then it is clearly a danger to the nation. The next two readings in this chapter present different views of the relationship between the riots and poverty.

Finally, does poverty have any good effects on the society? Are there any values or attitudes that have been preserved among the poor, for example, which are important for America to retain? The last article considers this.

Taken altogether, the selections in this chapter should help you to draw your own conclusions about the effect that poverty has on the poor, on those in the society who are not poor, and on the country itself.

1. MY HUSBAND GOT 5 TO 15 YEARS. *

There are several different ways in which crime and poverty may be linked. The following article describes one of them.

My husband is only 21. He was working at Whitaker Manufacturing Company as a machine operator. But he broke his hand before he was eligible for the insurance there. He went in on a Monday morning with his hand and tried to work, but they wouldn't let him.

We tried to get by. He tried to work through a day labor office, Ready Man, and even took the cast off himself to do it. We had to let a family take our two-year-old little boy temporarily.

Tom found out that the man was beating our son and we took him right back.

I guess Tom got frantic because of it and because I am expecting next month. Anyway, I can't claim what he did wasn't wrong.

First they caught him in a house he had broken into. Then, while he was out on bail, they caught him on a double armed robbery. He held up two cleaning stores.

It cost us $300 for bail and for the attorney just for the pre-trial hearing. It would have cost us $500 more for the trial, except we got a public defender. He told Tom to plead guilty.

He got 5 to 15 years. It was so much.

I want right now to get an attorney who will review the case. I will go to work right after I have the baby so I can pay him.

It was so much it couldn't be fair.

What Do You Think?

1. Was there anything that Tom could have done to meet the needs of his family other than turn to crime?
2. His wife said, "It [the verdict] was so much it couldn't be fair." Do you agree with her? How do you define "fair" in such a situation?
3. Might the verdict have been different if Tom could have afforded an outstanding lawyer? Explain.

---

* Excerpted from Kenan Heise, *They Speak for Themselves*. Chicago, Ill.: The Young Christian Workers, 1965. © 1965 by Kenan Heise. Used by permission.

2. THE FOURTH SUMMER: THE GRADY FAMILY *

The poor family must live at close quarters and must seek income wherever it can be found. What effect does this have on family life, attitude toward law, and education? These are questions raised by the following description of life among the migrant workers.

That fourth year up the road turned into the scrappingest season the Gradys ever spent. Addie could feel her tongue lash out and she couldn't stop herself. It wasn't only with Henry; her tongue sharpened with the children too. It was queer how that awful aching love you could have for a person could show itself only in hateful words.

The heat made things no better. That summer Pennsylvania and New York in July felt hotter than any place Addie remembered in Georgia or Florida. It was the kind of heat that laid a great weight on your arms and legs and took away every bit of tucker you ever had. In every single camp they went to all seven of them slept and dressed and cooked and ate in one room; when it was ten foot by fourteen, it was a big room.

They had running arguments.

They argued over should they open the door and the window and fight the flies or should they shut the door and the window and fight the heat. Whichever way they decided, it didn't make any difference; they found themselves fighting heat and flies and each other all at once.

They argued over should they specialize in beans or should they pick at anything that came along. Henry wanted to specialize; being a specialist, he said, gave a man dignity. Addie said who did he think he was? . . . All right, so if he was [the President] he could specialize in being President of the United States, but if he was Henry Grady he just better crawl along after whatever crop he could find that could use him. Time was Addie could say something like that in a tone that made it three-quarters gentle spoofing and one-quarter serious; now when she said it the words sounded one-quarter serious and three-quarters plain mean. And all the time she was saying them she yearned to take him in her arms and comfort him, but she never did.

They argued should they let the kids work in the fields. Most of the parents had their children work. It sure did add up to more pay

---

tickets when you did, and you couldn't say the extra money wasn't manna in the wilderness. Of course, some places you had to watch out for the inspector. There were special words you called out if you saw him coming, and everybody knew what the words meant; everybody, that is, but the inspector. Matthew thought this was a great joke, and he and Roosevelt set to figuring out a game. The children played it over and over again and taught it to the other kids every time they went to a different camp. The game went like this:

Roosevelt would shout, "Pickin' time," and all the children would drop to their knees on the ground and begin crawling along, making motions with their hands, pantomime-like, at picking beans, and they would singsong:

> *Pick* the ol' beans and *drop* 'em in the basket,
> *Pick* the ol' beans and *drop* 'em in the basket,

and all the while Roosevelt stood turning round and round with his hand shading his eyes, looking and looking at the edge of the sky, and then all of a sudden he'd yell, "Pick 'em clean, Joe," and every child would throw himself flat on the ground and bury his face in the dust. Then from nowhere would come Matthew limping along, dragging his poor clubfoot and managing to swagger and strut, and he and Roosevelt had a little conversation.

Matthew: "Hi, Mr. Row Boss."
Roosevelt: "Hi your own self, Mr. Inspector."
Matthew: "How's the beans, Mr. Row Boss?"
Roosevelt: "Not good, not bad, Mr. Inspector. Just about like they ought to be."
Matthew: "Any kids working here?"
Roosevelt: "Kids? What kids?" (Twisting his head in all directions.) "I don't see no kids. Do you?"
Matthew: "No, no kids. Thank you, Mr. Row Boss, sir, thank you, so long."

And Matthew would limp away; whereupon the little bean pickers would all jump up and race after him and tackle him and down he would go in a heap of tangled arms and legs.

Sometimes the dialogue would get more elaborate. They would discuss the weather in detail, walk up and down examining the bean plants, stepping carefully over the prostrate children, and they would inquire after the health of each other's wives and children.

The first time Addie saw them play it she thought it was cute; times after that a notion nagged at her that it might not be just right for children to be playing at cheating the law. But what was right and wrong anyway? What was the law? Some places there was a law and inspectors and children weren't supposed to work; or sometimes it seemed to be all right if they worked until they were twelve or fourteen and then they had to go to town and get working papers; other places it was all legal no matter how young or old they were. If the law was the law, why didn't it work one place the same as another?

Henry said children ought to work. It wasn't good to leave them back in camp alone, and besides, it was a healthy thing for kids to work, beans or onions or crops like that or picking up potatoes after the machine. They couldn't begin too young, and it was a sure thing they had to learn what it was like because they'd never have a chance to do anything else all their lives long.

This was when Addie really sounded off. So they wouldn't ever have a chance to do anything else, would they? Well, her children weren't going to grow up to be nothing but stooping, crawling bean pickers on the season. They were going to get educated, never you mind how; they were going to train for something good and real, something where you wore a necktie or a uniform and used your head along with or maybe instead of your hands and stood up straight behind a counter or carried a tray or walked a beat or sat down in a chair with four legs in front of a desk and wrote words plain and clear on a typewriting machine. They were going to be somebody and they were going to belong somewhere.

Right there to her astonishment and chagrin Addie found herself crying. Henry said, "Hey, there," and looked so stricken that Addie said, still cross, "Oh, all right, so you're so crazy about having them pick, let them pick, but only just so long as there isn't any school around for them to go to. When we get to a camp where regular school's going on in town and the bus comes by, or where there's one of those summer schools for migrant kids, then they're going to school, understand? No more picking!"

*   *   *   *   *

Way back in the spring down in Florida they'd argued over which crew leader to join up with. Henry wanted to go with Digger. Two summers ago they had traveled with him, and he had really rooked them good; couldn't Henry remember that? How he'd promised them 75¢ a hamper for beans, and when the time came he said sure, he was paying 75¢ a hamper, but he had to take out 20¢ for his own share for getting them the job and 5¢ to pay on what they owed him for supplying food all the way up (that food was nothing but soda pop and crackers and sausage and cold baked beans out of a can) and for giving them credit at the camp store before the work began (six days it was, because of the steady rain, before the heat wave brought on the beans in a rush). And he charged them a dollar apiece when they crossed the James River ferry from Little Creek to Kiptopeke when everybody knew it was just 86¢ a person, and when they complained he said if you don't like it you know what you can do. And when they ended up the season with no money at all, he claimed they still owed some (Addie was convinced they didn't but she had no proof) but they were such good people, he said, he'd just forget it. Rubbish!

This year he'd promised them a camp like a motel, with a real "rec" room and television and a cook truck that went right into the fields every noon with hot lunches. "And how much would he take out of our pay for all that?" asked Addie tartly. Henry persisted. Digger had got himself two buses this year to transport his crew; bus riding, said Henry, was sure a whole lot more comfortable than traveling in the back of a truck.

Digger owned an electric razor and he dressed flashy. He was a sweet talker and slick, and when Henry listened to him he forgot all about the crooked treatment of two years back. Henry was just like a child. The very sight of Digger put Addie's back up; as for Digger, he kept a wide berth from Addie. "He knows I see through him," she said to herself.

There were other reasons, too, why Addie didn't want the family to get tied up with Digger. He had a roving eye, and his eye had lit on Lottie. In the four years she'd been on the road with them Lottie had come to be a right pretty eighteen. She fitted nice into the family.

* * * * *

No, they did right to stay away from Digger's outfit and stick with Cap.

The beans were running good, and soon there would be potatoes. The Gradys settled into the camp routine. Up at five, get the family stirring, send Roosevelt out to stand in line at the nearest spigot and fetch a bucket of water, heat up some wash water and last night's coffee, get the grits cooking. (A good thing they'd brought along that little old oilstove and didn't have to crowd into the cook shanty and fight for a spot on a wood-burning cookstove.) Lottie took charge of Princess Anne, bathed and dressed her and fixed her some powdered milk with a little coffee in it. Roosevelt and Sister spread up sandwiches for lunch, and somehow everybody got some breakfast down and turned up ready for the truck at six.

They worked for half a dozen different growers, and sometimes they had to ride forty, fifty, seventy-five miles to get to the fields. Then it was kneel and pick and pick and pick; change to a crouch and pick and pick; go back to kneeling and crawling; get your hamper full, collect your ticket and stuff it deep down good into your pocket, back again to pick, pick, pick. If you stopped to rest, you only felt hotter and stiffer when you started in again.

On the ride coming back the truck would stop at a roadside stand where they had a little store and the people would pour out and cash their bean tickets for cans and cold cuts and cookies. Addie liked to get potatoes and onions and canned tomatoes and pork butts and stew them all together in a kettle; sometimes it was neck bones and rice and black-eyed peas. Canned mackerel with cabbage and corned bread was good too. One night Addie would get dinner and Lottie would do the family wash, and the next night they would trade chores. Evenings there was nothing, just nothing to do but sit in the doorway or on the ground looking for a breath of air that wasn't there, till you got sleepy enough to fall on a straw-stuffed mattress and go out like a light, not caring was the window open or shut.

The heat hung on.

What Do You Think?

1. Will the Grady children ever get to school? Is Addie's dream of their working in jobs where they can wear a tie or a uniform a reasonable one? Explain.
2. In what ways was poverty the cause of the family quarrels? Does having the whole family living together in one room make it a more closely knit unit or divide it? What evidence can you find in the story to support your answers?
3. What lessons about laws are the Grady children learning?

3.   LET AMERICA BE AMERICA AGAIN *

There is a contrast between the America that the poor are told about and dream of and the America that is a reality to them. The black poet Langston Hughes wrote of this contrast in the poem that follows.

Let America be America again.
Let it be the dream it used to be.
Let it be the pioneer on the plain
Seeking a home where he himself is free.

(America never was America to me.)

Let America be the dream the dreamers dreamed—
Let it be that great strong land of love

---

* Reprinted by permission of Harold Ober Associates, Inc. Copyright 1938 by Langston Hughes. Renewed.

Where never kings connive nor tyrants scheme
That any man be crushed by one above.

(It never was America to me.)

O, let my land be a land where Liberty
Is crowned with no false patriotic wreath,
But opportunity is real, and life is free,
Equality is in the air we breathe.

(There's never been equality for me,
Nor freedom in this "homeland of the free.")

Say who are you that mumbles in the dark?
And who are you that draws your veil across the stars?

I am the poor white, fooled and pushed apart,
I am the Negro bearing slavery's scars.
I am the red man driven from the land,
I am the immigrant clutching the hope I seek—
And finding only the same old stupid plan.
Of dog eat dog, of mighty crush the weak.

I am the young man, full of strength and hope,
Tangled in that ancient endless chain
Of profit, power, gain, of grab the land!
Of grab the gold! Of grab the ways of satisfying need!
Of work the men! Of take the pay!
Of owning everything for one's own greed!

I am the farmer, bondsman to the soil.
I am the worker sold to the machine.
I am the Negro, servant to you all.
I am the people, worried, hungry, mean—
Hungry yet today despite the dream.
Beaten yet today—O Pioneers!
I am the man who never got ahead,
The poorest worker bartered through the years.

Yet I'm the one who dreamt our basic dream
In that Old World while still a serf of kings,
Who dreamt a dream so strong, so brave, so true,
That even yet its mighty daring sings
In every brick and stone, in every furrow turned

That's made America the land it has become.
O, I'm the man who sailed those early seas
In search of what I meant to be my home—
For I'm the one who left dark Ireland's shore,
And Poland's plain, and England's grassy lea,
And torn from Black Africa's strand I came
To build a "homeland of the free."

The free?

A dream—
Still beckoning to me!

O, let America be America again—
The land that never has been yet—
And yet must be—
The land where *every* man is free.
The land that's mine—
The poor man's, Indian's, Negro's, ME—
Who made America,
Whose sweat and blood, whose faith and pain,
Whose hand at the foundry, whose plow in the rain,
Must bring back our mighty dream again.

Sure, call me any ugly name you choose—
The steel of freedom does not stain.
From those who live like leeches on the people's lives,
We must take back our land again,
America!

O, yes,
I say it plain,
America never was America to me,
And yet I swear this oath—
America will be!
An ever-living seed,
Its dream
Lies deep in the heart of me.

We, the people, must redeem
Our land, the mines, the plants, the rivers,
The mountains and the endless plain—
All, all the stretch of these great green states—
And make America again!

What Do You Think?

1. When the poet used the word "America," was he referring to a place or to an idea? What evidence can you find?

2. The poet says:
   "I am the people, worried, hungry, mean—
   Hungry yet today despite the dream.
   Beaten yet today—O Pioneers!
   I am the man who never got ahead,
   The poorest worker bartered through the years."
   This poem was written during the Depression. Would it be any different if written today?

3. Are there any ways in which the feelings about poverty and lack of opportunity expressed in this poem could hurt the society? Explain.

4. SEVEN MARKS OF POVERTY *

If poverty only affected the lives, attitudes, and institutions of the poor, that would be serious enough, but it does more. The following article describes seven ways in which poverty puts its mark on the entire society.

Poverty among almost a fifth of our people is both root and offshoot of inadequate schooling, deficient health services, crime and juvenile delinquency, inadequate social security and welfare programs to deal with the problems of broken homes and the penury of so many of the old, indecent housing conditions, civil strife, and high unemployment resulting in the main from slow economic growth.

For one thing, this: Today, with an estimated 16 million children among the families of the poor, parents everywhere are discovering that children from urban or rural slums bring the scars of their poverty when they enter the schools. Without pride—or cause for pride—in their backgrounds, they carry indifference and destructiveness. They bring the limited vocabulary of their unschooled parents. They have trouble understanding the teaching. Through their impact upon other children, all of us pay the bill for long neglect. In addition, youths aged 16 and over are more than three times as likely to leave school when the family income is under $5,000 as when it is $7,500 or higher.

---

* Excerpted from Leon H. Keyserling, *Progress or Poverty: The U. S. at the Crossroads.* Washington, D. C.: Conference on Economic Progress, 1964.

For a second thing, this: If anyone proposed a scheme to put out of action one-third of the young men who might be needed to defend the nation, he would probably be tried for treason. Yet, Selective Service reported in 1963 that *half* of the young men taking the pre-induction tests had failed. The causes were physical or intellectual deficiencies, or both. President Kennedy appointed a task force to study the facts. It found that, even if all our young men who became 18 in 1962 had taken the tests, *one-third* would probably have failed. Among the sample group of rejectees studied, eight out of ten were school dropouts, and half of these had left school to help support their families; almost half of those who failed to pass the intelligence test came from families with six or more children. The rate of unemployment was about double the rate for all men in the same age group. And most of the young men who failed lost almost their last chance to get the training and discipline, by customary methods, necessary for many industrial jobs. They thus lost their chance to break out of poverty.

For a third thing, this: Some areas of our growing cities are unsafe for women and children even during the daytime, and unsafe for all at night. Crimes of violence of all types are perpetrated largely by those whose early years have been thwarted by poverty or deprivation. Involuntary idleness turns many toward social aberration. And juvenile delinquency increases as the economically handicapped children drop out of school and fail to find work. . . .

For a fourth thing, this: Poverty and all its burdens are highly concentrated among those who must be helped by social programs, because in the very nature of things most of them cannot help themselves— children in broken homes, young female heads of families who cannot work or earn much if they do, and above all, in the tragedy of their penury, millions of our senior citizens. . .

For a fifth thing, this: Poverty frequently means living under slum conditions, whether in big cities or on the farms. It means overcrowding and lack of privacy; sharing plumbing facilities with scores of others; unique exposure to disease and mental breakdown, with no money to call the doctor; paying more rent than the family can afford; exploitation by high-pressure salesmen who force upon them cars and home furnishings at usurious interest rates and often repossess them. And these living conditions drive children into the streets. There, in addition to all else, more fortunate neighbors may treat them with scorn, blame them for their wretchedness, and cut down their self-respect.

For a sixth thing, this: . . . Just so long as poverty and unemployment are so highly concentrated among Negroes and other minority groups, it is only reasonable to anticipate that a quality of desperation will continue to attach to the Negro's appeal to the conscience of his fellow citizens. Civil rights laws, granted their imperative necessity, do .

not in themselves create additional jobs nor reduce poverty. And just so long as people of different-colored skins have to compete for the scant jobs which mean food and shelter, we'll go on having racial tensions.⌋

And for a seventh thing, this: Apart from the other separate factors in poverty, but both root and offshoot of them all, is the chronically high rate of unemployment.

What Do You Think?

1. The author talks of the impact which the presence of children of the poor in a class has on other school children and of the scorn with which these poorer children are treated by people who are more fortunate than they. Does this suggest that there should be separate schools just for poor children so that they would not have to mix with others? Are there advantages to this idea? Disadvantages?

2. In recent years the standards for admission into the armed forces have been changed so that young men with poverty backgrounds can be taken in and given a chance to make up their deficiencies while serving. What do you think of this idea?

3. Do the poor really have a "unique exposure to disease and mental breakdown"? Explain your reasoning.

5. VIOLENCE IN OUR MAJOR CITIES *

The United States has been hit by a series of riots in poorer areas of its cities ever since 1963. What is the cause of these riots? Is it poverty? Racism? Both? Senator Robert Byrd of West Virginia gave his opinion in a speech on the Senate floor.

Mr. President, the violence sweeping through our major cities today is appalling, to say the very least.

Peace-loving Americans everywhere are being forced to bear witness to the spectacle of screaming mobs running through the streets, looting stores, burning buildings and cars, and killing innocent citizens.

In Newark, Plainfield, Boston, Tampa, Los Angeles, Chicago, and Cleveland, to name just a few cities, this mad anarchy has become like a cancer.

---

* Excerpted from the *Congressional Record,* 90th Congress, First Session, Senate, July 18, 1967, p. S 9906.

How tragic it is to read of the heroic fire captain in Newark who, responding on a call in the line of duty, was met by a hail of sniper fire. That courageous man made repeated attempts under fire to carry out his duty.

How equally sad it was to read of the little boy in Plainfield, N. J., shot accidentally by a policeman who, wounded and helpless himself, was being stomped to death by a blood-hungry and hate-filled mob.

These horrible stories sound so very much out of place in America.

We hear the usual excuses for the riots. They are the same excuses that were trotted out in the wake of the Watts riot. The ghettos are blamed; yet, people of all races have lived in ghettos in the past, but they have not rioted.

Poverty is blamed for the riots; yet poverty-stricken whites outnumber poverty-stricken Negroes in America, but they are not rioting. Moreover, there are millions of poor but upstanding Negro citizens who deplore violence and disorder and who do not subscribe to riots.

If living in poverty reposes in one a duty or a right to riot, then Abraham Lincoln would have been the Stokely Carmichael of his day.

Discrimination, we hear, is back of the riots; yet, millions of lowly immigrants have come to this country, immigrants who could not even speak the English language and who were thus placed at an additional great disadvantage.

The Lebanese, the Germans, the Italians, the Poles, the Greeks, the Jews, and others—they too were discriminated against, but they did not react with violence in the streets.

They also lived in ghettos but they kept their ghettos clean. Their ghettos did not become slums.

The immigrants reacted to the discrimination against them in a totally different way. When they could not find work, they created it by setting up their own little shops. Their ghettos did not become slums. They became homes, where they gave thanks for what they had earned. These immigrants did not believe that they had a right to demand handouts, nor did they believe that they had a right to plunder or to burn or to destroy or to kill.

Eradicate the slums, we are told, and this will prevent riots. Yet, Watts was not a slum. Slums are not built. They develop as a result of the careless living of people—people who throw their trash in the hallways and on the stairways, into the yards, and onto the streets. If people are irresponsible and dirty in their way of living, and have no desire to put forth the effort to improve their surroundings, then we will have slums with slovenly people residing in them.

For years I lived in the coal-mining communities of West Virginia. I recall the depression of the 1930's. Poverty was everywhere. It was everyone's companion. Yet, West Virginians, whether white or Negro, did not riot. They were law-abiding citizens, as they are today. One may explain, "But there were no large urban ghettos." True. But there was poverty—grinding poverty. That was before the days of collective bargaining, social security, and welfare checks or even unemployment compensation. Yet, those people did not burn and plunder and loot and engage in mass anarchy. They believed in an orderly society. And even though they were poor, most of them, Negro and white, were not willing to leave their floors unscrubbed or a step unrepaired. Of course, there were no plumbing fixtures to worry about.

Many of those poor people, white and Negro alike, took pride in their surroundings. Their floors were clean, their yards were clean. Here and there they planted a flower or a piece of shrubbery.

And, best of all, white and Negro, they got along well together. If a Negro became unable to work, whites and Negroes would try to help. If a white miner became ill or was injured in the mines, Negroes and whites would try to help. There were many times when I, as a meatcutter or produce clerk in the company store, placed a large flour barrel at the end of the meat counter and started a "pounding" for a sick Negro miner or a sick white miner. At the end of the day, the barrel would be filled with flour, meal, bacon, pinto beans, and other provisions and ready to deliver to the stricken family.

So, Mr. President, people may be poor and, yet, considerate of others. They may live in poverty and yet take pride in their humble surroundings. Poverty neither provides a license for laziness nor for lawlessness.

We can take the people out of the slums, but we cannot take the slums out of the people. Wherever some people go, the ratholes will follow. Wherever some people go, the slums will follow. All the housing, and all the welfare programs conceivable, will not stop the riots or do away with the slums. People first have to clean up inside themselves. They must stop tearing off the wallpaper, breaking the windows, ripping up the bannisters and the stairs, and destroying the plumbing fixtures of rented properties before they can properly take care of their own. The rats will not be kept away as long as the garbage is tossed into the yard instead of into the garbage can.

Moreover, men will not deserve or enjoy the respect and approbation of their fellows except by earning it. It cannot be acquired in any other way. They will be largely judged by their conduct. If they conduct themselves in an orderly way, they will not have to worry about police brutality. If they obey the laws, the laws will protect them. But a government of laws cannot tolerate disrespect for, and violation of its laws. To do so would herald the first evidence of society's decay.

I am sure that I speak the thoughts of many of my fellow West Virginians, and millions of my fellow Americans, both white and Negro, when I say that we cannot stand idly by and tolerate the shameful rape of democracy.

Those who choose to step outside the law must be punished. And those who insist upon force must be met with a greater force. Mobs must not be permitted to prevail.

Perhaps it is spontaneous madness which erupts into some of these riots. A police arrest, properly made, in the line of duty, and to enforce the law, draws a jeering and taunting crowd. Bricks are thrown. The police are subjected to verbal and physical abuse, and then a twisted rumor moves about the neighborhood. The final result is a full-scale display of vicious mob savagery which cripples or destroys everything in its mad path.

One could not rightly say that these twisted rumors are the work of outside instigators in all cases, but certainly the seeds of violence are often fertilized and nurtured by a minority of outside agitators overtly and covertly active in fomenting hate and racial strife.

What Do You Think?

1. What did Senator Byrd mean when he suggested: "If living in poverty reposes in one a duty or a right to riot, then Abraham Lincoln would have been the Stokely Carmichael of his day."? Is Senator Byrd omitting any factors in his comparison?

2. What effect would it have on a big city slum apartment house if one family which had previously been careless in its living habits started being very careful and clean?

3. To what kind of agitators is Senator Byrd referring? What would be their goal?

4. Would you agree that "we can take the people out of the slums but we cannot take the slums out of people"? Why or why not? What does this saying mean?

6. WHAT ARE THE CAUSES OF RIOTS? *

Senator Byrd rejects poverty and racism as sufficient explanations for the riots and suggests some alternatives. The 1967 riot in Newark, New Jersey, was one that had prompted his speech. A special presidential commission investigated and reported on the outbreak of that

---

* Excerpted from the *Report of the National Advisory Commission on Civil Disorders*. Washington, D. C.: U. S. Government Printing Office, 1968.

*riot and the typical riot participant. Does this report confirm or deny
the Senator's contentions about the relationship between poverty and
racism and the riots?*

Newark

Founded in 1666, the city, a part of the Greater New York City
port complex, rises from the salt marshes of the Passaic River. Although
in 1967 Newark's population of 400,000 still ranked it thirtieth among
American municipalities, for the past 20 years the white middle class
had been deserting the city for the suburbs.

In the late 1950's, the desertions had become a rout. Between 1960
and 1967, the city lost a net total of more than 70,000 white residents.
Replacing them in vast areas of dilapidated housing where living conditions, according to a prominent member of the County Bar Association,
were so bad that "people would be kinder to their pets," were Negro
migrants, Cubans, and Puerto Ricans. In 6 years, the city switched from
65 per cent white to 52 per cent Negro and 10 per cent Puerto Rican
and Cuban.

The white population, nevertheless, retained political control of the
city. On both the city council and the board of education, seven of nine
members were white. In other key boards, the disparity was equal or
greater. In the central ward [where the city government planned to clear
150 acres of the ghetto and let the state build a new medical and dental
college despite the opposition of the Negro residents], the Negro con-
stituents and their white councilman found themselves on opposite sides
of almost every crucial issue.

The municipal administration lacked the ability to respond quickly
enough to navigate the swiftly changing currents. Even had it had great
astuteness, it would have lacked the financial resources to affect signifi-
cantly the course of events.

[After describing the way in which the flight of the white middle
class from the city had cut down on its ability to collect taxes to meet
its needs, the *Report* continues.]

Consequently, there was less money to spend on education. Newark's
per capita outlay on schools was considerably less than that of surround-
ing communities. Yet within the city's school system were 78,000 children,
14,000 more than 10 years earlier.

Twenty thousand pupils were on double sessions. The dropout rate
was estimated to be as high as 33 per cent. Of 13,600 Negroes between
the ages of 16 and 19, more than 6,000 were not in school. In 1960
over half of the adult Negro population had less than an eighth grade education.

The typical ghetto cycle of high unemployment, family breakup, and crime was present in all its elements. Approximately 12 per cent of Negroes were without jobs. An estimated 40 per cent of Negro children lived in broken homes. Although Newark maintained proportionately the largest police force of any major city, its crime rate was among the highest in the Nation. In narcotics violations it ranked fifth nationally. Almost 80 per cent of the crimes were committed within 2 miles of the core of the city, where the central ward is located. A majority of the criminals were Negro. Most of the victims, likewise, were Negro. The Mafia was reputed to control much of the organized crime.

Under such conditions a major segment of the Negro population became increasingly militant. Largely excluded from positions of traditional political power, Negroes, tutored by a handful of militant social activists who had moved into the city in the early 1960's, made use of the antipoverty program, in which poor people were guaranteed representation, as a political springboard. This led to friction between the United Community Corporation, the agency that administered the antipoverty program, and the city administration.

When it became known that the secretary of the board of education intended to retire, the militants proposed for the position the city's budget director, a Negro with a master's degree in accounting. The mayor, however, had already nominated a white man. Since the white man had only a high school education, and at least 70 per cent of the children in the school system were Negro, the issue of who was to obtain the secretaryship, an important and powerful position, quickly became a focal issue.

Joined with the issue of the 150-acre medical school site, the area of which had been expanded to triple the original request—an expansion regarded by the militants as an effort to dilute black political power by moving out Negro residents—the board of education battle resulted in a confrontation between the mayor and the militants. Both sides refused to alter their positions.

Into this impasse stepped a Washington Negro named Albert Roy Osborne. A flamboyant, 42-year-old former wig salesman who called himself Colonel Hassan Jeru-Ahmed and wore a black beret, he presided over a mythical "Blackman's Volunteer Army of Liberation." Articulate and magnetic, the self-commissioned "colonel" proved to be a one-man show. He brought Negro residents flocking to board of education and planning board meetings. The colonel spoke in violent terms, and backed his words with violent action. At one meeting he tore the tape from the official stenographic recorder. . . .

It became more and more evident to the militants that, though they might not be able to prevail, they could prevent the normal transaction of business. . . .

On June 27th, when a new secretary to the board of education was to be named, the state police set up a command post in the Newark armory.

The militants, led by the local CORE (Congress of Racial Equality) chapter, disrupted and took over the board of education meeting. The outcome was a stalemate. The incumbent secretary decided to stay on another year. No one was satisfied.

At the beginning of July there were 24,000 unemployed Negroes within the city limits. Their ranks were swelled by an estimated 20,000 teenagers, many of whom, with school out and the summer recreation program curtailed due to a lack of funds, had no place to go.

On July 8, Newark and East Orange Police attempted to disperse a group of Black Muslims. In the melee that followed, several police officers and Muslims suffered injuries necessitating medical treatment. The resulting charges and countercharges heightened the tension between police and Negroes.

Early on the evening of July 12, a cabdriver named John Smith began, according to police reports, tailgating a Newark police car. Smith was an unlikely candidate to set a riot in motion. Forty years old, a Georgian by birth, he had attended college for a year before entering the Army in 1950. In 1953 he had been honorably discharged with the rank of corporal. A chess-playing trumpet player, he had worked as a musician and a factory hand before, in 1963, becoming a cabdriver.

As a cabdriver, he appeared to be a hazard. Within a relatively short period of time he had eight or nine accidents. His license was revoked. When, with a woman passenger in his cab, he was stopped by the police, he was in violation of that revocation.

From the high-rise towers of the Reverend William P. Hayes housing project, the residents can look down on the orange-red brick facade of the Fourth Precinct Police Station and observe every movement. Shortly after 9:30 P.M., people saw Smith, who either refused or was unable to walk, being dragged out of a police car and into the front door of the station.

Within a few minutes at least two civil rights leaders received calls from a hysterical woman declaring a cabdriver was being beaten by the police. When one of the persons at the station notified the cab company of Smith's arrest, cabdrivers all over the city began learning of it over their cab radios.

A crowd formed on the grounds of the housing project across the narrow street from the station. As more and more people arrived, the description of the beating purportedly administered to Smith became more and more exaggerated. The descriptions were supported by other complaints of police malpractice that, over the years, had been submitted for investigation—but had never been heard of again.

Several Negro community leaders, telephoned by a civil rights worker and informed of the deteriorating situation, rushed to the scene. By 10:15 P.M. the atmosphere had become so potentially explosive that Kenneth Melchior, the senior police inspector on the night watch, was called. He arrived at approximately 10:30 P.M.

Met by a delegation of civil rights leaders and militants who requested the right to see and interview Smith, Inspector Melchior acceded to their request.

When the delegation was taken to Smith, Melchior agreed with their observations that, as a result of injuries Smith had suffered, he needed to be examined by a doctor. Arrangements were made to have a police car transport him to the hospital.

Both within and outside of the police station, the atmosphere was electric with hostility. Carloads of police officers arriving for the 10:45 P.M. change of shifts were subjected to a gauntlet of catcalls, taunts, and curses.

Joined by Oliver Lofton, administrative director of the Newark Legal Services Project, the Negro community leaders inside the station requested an interview with Inspector Melchior. As they were talking to the inspector about initiating an investigation to determine how Smith had been injured, the crowd outside became more and more unruly. Two of the Negro spokesmen went outside to attempt to pacify the people.

There was little reaction to the spokesmen's appeal that the people go home. The second of the two had just finished speaking from atop a car when several Molotov cocktails smashed against the wall of the police station.

The Profile of the Rioter

The typical rioter in the summer of 1967 was a Negro, unmarried male between the ages of 15 and 24. He was in many ways different from the stereotype. He was not a migrant. He was born in the state and was a lifelong resident of the city in which the riot took place. Economically his position was about the same as his Negro neighbors who did not actively participate in the riot.

Although he had not, usually, graduated from high school, he was somewhat better educated than the average inner-city Negro, having at least attended high school for a time.

Nevertheless, he was more likely to be working in a menial or low-status job as an unskilled laborer. If he was employed, he was not working full time and his employment was frequently interrupted by periods of unemployment.

He feels strongly that he deserves a better job and that he is barred from achieving it, not because of lack of training, ability, or ambition, but because of discrimination by employers.

He rejects the white bigot's stereotype of the Negro as ignorant and shiftless. He takes great pride in his race and he believes that in some respects Negroes are superior to whites. He is extremely hostile to whites, but his hostility is more apt to be a product of social and economic class than of race; he is almost equally hostile toward middle-class Negroes.

He is substantially better informed about politics than Negroes who were not involved in the riots. He is more likely to be actively engaged in civil rights efforts, but he is extremely distrustful of the political system and of political leaders.

*   *   *   *   *

[In describing the typical counter-rioter (those who urged rioters to "cool-it"), the report states that, "he was considerably better educated and more affluent than either the rioter or the noninvolved."]

What Do You Think?

1. Was poverty a major cause of the Newark riot? Was it *the* major cause? What evidence can you find in the articles on riots to support your answers?
2. Do poor people have a right to disobey a law if they feel that it is unfair to them? Explain.

7. YESTERDAY'S PEOPLE *

Up to this point all of the articles in this chapter have focused on harmful or allegedly harmful effects of poverty. Are there any good effects? Are there, for example, any behavior patterns or values that poor people have that more affluent Americans might profit from? The following article describes some of the values of the poor in Appalachia.

Never have I seen a mountaineer "lording it over" another because he has a new car or a new job or a new house. This kind of materialism is completely rejected. Mountaineers want to have their status based not on objects but on their individuality within their own group.

*   *   *   *   *

There is an offhand attitude toward money, almost as if it did not matter, which is in strong contrast to the middle-class striving for money

* Excerpted from Jack E. Weller, *Yesterday's People: Life in Contemporary Appalachia.* Lexington, Ky.: University of Kentucky Press, 1965. Copyright © The University of Kentucky Press. Used by permission.

as a goal in itself. Having a certain amount of money obviously does matter, since life itself depends on it, but I have seldom seen a mountaineer who seemed to care how much he was able to get or to save. Other things are much more important to him.

A similar disregard for time is also part of the mountain man's make-up. He lives by rhythms other than the hour, day or week. The rhythms of the shifts at the mine, of hunting and fishing seasons, of gardening—these provide the paces for his life. The particular hour of the day is of less concern to him than it is to the middle-class person.

His person-orientation makes him much more aware of his person-to-person relationships than of a time schedule which must be kept. He cares far more about keeping a friendly relationship with a neighbor whom he has met on the way to a meeting than about being there on time. This is one very important point that middle-class persons must be aware of as they have dealings with mountain people. In the middle-class world, a man can impersonally do what business needs to be done with a person, then proceed elsewhere. In the folk culture, you don't just stop in for a moment to check on a detail or two of business, then move on. Each contact is a person-to-person encounter, and this takes time—hours of it. A trip to the store, going to the neighbors' to borrow a cup of sugar or an ax, meeting a friend on the road—these are not impersonal encounters, in which the business at hand can be done quickly, but are occasions for the kind of personal relationships that form the very core of the mountain man's existence.

A county school official recently discussed his efforts to see three men who were being chosen for a special training program. It took him six hours, because—as he noted—"you can't do business with these people on a time schedule." You must also "set a spell," and in the midst of this person-to-person meeting any business you may have can be done. The impersonal manner of business dealing common to the middle class simply will not do for the mountaineer.

What Do You Think?

1. Are these characteristics peculiar to mountaineers or are they characteristics of poor people in general? Have you encountered people with these characteristics?

2. What effect would it have on the society if these attitudes disappeared from it? If they were adopted by all?

3. Are these attitudes the result of the mountaineers' poverty or a cause of it? Explain.

ACTIVITIES FOR INVOLVEMENT

1. Review all the readings in Chapters 3 and 4 as well as in this chapter, looking for evidence on the relationship between poverty and family life. Decide if poverty has any effect upon the family. Write a paper supporting your conclusion.

2. A judge in Washington, D. C., remarked: "From my own experience, I know that most of the defendants convicted of crimes of violence in the District of Columbia are indigent. A successful war on poverty would come close to solving the crime problem." Collect all the articles on crime in your local newspaper for one week. Study them and then tell whether they tend to support the judge's idea or contradict it.

3. Which *three* of the following would be most affected by poverty that exists in the society? In what ways?
   a. A middle-class suburban housewife.
   b. A wealthy businessman.
   c. A teacher in a rural school.
   d. A teenage girl living in a luxury apartment in the center of a city.
   e. A policeman assigned to patrol duty in a city.
   f. A young man eligible for the draft.
Be prepared to defend your choices.

4. The America that Langston Hughes talked about in his poem was proclaimed in the Declaration of Independence, the Preamble to the Constitution, the Bill of Rights, and other great American documents. Refer to these documents and list the statements which describe this "America." Which of the ideals have we come closest to achieving? Which have we still to accomplish? Is the existence of poverty contrary to these ideals? Explain.

5. Senator Byrd's speech was made after the Newark riot but before the publication of the *Report of the National Advisory Commission on Civil Disorders* from which the description of the beginning of that riot was taken. Hold a discussion to see if the class can agree as to what parts of the speech he would have changed if the *Report* had been available and what parts he would have kept the same.

6. Study a comic strip such as "L'il Abner" or a television program such as "The Beverly Hillbillies." Report on the extent to which they present the contrast between mountain and middle-class values that is discussed in the last article. What is funny? Who are the heroes? Why are they so popular?

What Can We Do About Poverty?

If poverty has so many effects upon the poor and upon the entire society and almost all of them are bad, what can and should be done about it? Can poverty be eliminated or at least lessened? If so, how?

There are people who argue that if we were really serious about doing something about poverty, we would have succeeded in eliminating it by now. Some even believe that the affluent majority in America wish to preserve poverty. One says:

In present day America, the middle class is defined largely by the fact that the poor exist. Doctors are middle class, but so are bookkeepers; factory workers vacation with lawyers, drive bigger cars than teachers, live next door to store-owners, and send their children to school with the children of bank tellers. In a middle class so diffuse, with almost no characteristic common to all, middle-class income, education, and housing are what the poor do not have. If the present poor should become middle class, no meaning would remain to that phrase. . . . The middle class knows that the economists are right when they say that poverty can be eliminated if we only will it; they simply do not will it.[1]

Can this be true? How can we tell? One possible way is to look at the existing welfare and antipoverty programs to see whether they are

---

[1] Excerpted from Adam Walinsky, "Keeping the Poor in Their Place: Notes on the Importance of Being One Up," Arthur B. Shostak and William Gomberg, eds., *New Perspectives on Poverty*. Englewood Cliffs, N. J.: Prentice-Hall, Inc., 1965.

really designed to do something about poverty or just to solve enough of the problems of the poor to keep them quiet and out of sight. A second way is to look at programs that have been proposed but not yet enacted, some proposed by scholars and politicians, others by the poor themselves, and then decide whether we, as members of the society, wish to support them.

Actions currently going on in the field of poverty can be divided into two categories: welfare and antipoverty. Although the line between these two groups is not always very clear and there are some activities that can be listed in both, there is a fundamental difference. Welfare actions are actions designed to solve specific problems of poor people. Giving enough food to someone who is hungry is a welfare action, as is providing shelter for a homeless family. The problems may be solved but the people are still poor after the action has been taken. Antipoverty activities are ones designed to bring individuals and groups out of poverty and into the mainstream of American affluence.

1.   WELFARE: PROBLEMS AND POSSIBILITIES

Private and religious organizations and individuals have been involved in welfare operations in America since early colonial days. Large scale governmental activity in this field, however, is a Twentieth Century phenomenon. Here are some things that are being done:

There are today dozens of federal laws and hundreds of state and local ones providing for welfare assistance. The total expenditure for governmental welfare programs passed the six billion dollar mark in 1966 and has been rising rapidly ever since then. The federal government provides more than 50 per cent of the funds.

Most of the federal programs provide assistance for people who are unable to take care of themselves for some obvious reason. The largest federal program, for example, is Aid to Families with Dependent Children, or ADC. Under this program the federal government gives grants to states, and the states distribute the money among families in which the parents cannot, for one reason or another, meet the needs of the children. If there is an able-bodied male in the household, the family is unlikely to receive aid. This feature has made ADC the target of frequent criticism. For example:

While the law concerning Aid to Dependent Children was originated as a means of supporting children when the head of the family cannot, the prevalent interpretation among the poor is that a family can only receive adequate assistance if the family head deserts.

An unskilled restaurant employee lives apart from his East

Harlem family and dodges their case worker so his family can collect full welfare benefits without deductions for his $65-a-week salary. "We have seven kids," he said. "Welfare don't give enough."

Mrs. Esther Medina, a mother of two from Monterey, Mexico, . . . said her husband had worked steadily until he arrived in New York City.

"He was not working and the men on the corners told him he would have to leave home so his family could get welfare. Welfare should not make men desert their families," she said.[2]

Those who support this interpretation of ADC charge that unless it is enforced men will refuse to work and will, instead, live off the payments made to their children.

Other federal programs involve aid to such groups as the blind, the crippled, and the elderly. These programs are carried out by the Department of Health, Education and Welfare.

People who do not fit into any of these federal categories must depend upon state and local governments for funds. Welfare benefits in the most generous states, primarily those in the northeast, are several times as high as those in the most niggardly ones, like Mississippi. Officials in the higher benefit states have expressed the suspicion that the other states deliberately keep benefits low to encourage the unemployables to move out. This compounds the problems of the states which make larger payments.

Recipient families often receive funds from several different programs. Since the different programs are run according to a variety of rules and one program may be made more or less liberal while others remain the same, recipients are often completely unable to understand why they receive as much (or as little!) as they do and suspect that someone is cheating them. The lives of some welfare recipients in New York City, whose welfare provisions are among the most generous in the nation, were described in the article "Life on Welfare" in Chapter 3. The articles "No Light and No Gas" and "You've Got to Eat Well" in the same chapter involve conditions of welfare clients in Chicago.

The welfare recipients in those selections seemed quite helpless. Other clients have, in recent years, become more aggressive in asserting their right to improved treatment and benefits. Typical of these is the group of Boston women who organized MAW, or Mothers for Adequate Welfare, in the summer of 1968.

On July 1, 1968, responsibility for welfare programs in Massachusetts

---

[2] Excerpted from Thomas A. Johnson, "Life on Welfare," *The New York Times,* December 19, 1966. © 1966 by The New York Times Company. Reprinted by permission.

was transferred from city governments to the state. The mothers in MAW undertook a series of actions designed to call attention to the inadequacy of their benefits and to the fact that some offices gave higher benefits than others to people in comparable circumstances even though all were now under state control. They demanded higher clothing and food allowances for their children. They also demanded telephones so that they would be able to call doctors or police stations in times of emergency rather than going out on dangerous nighttime streets to try to find the needed help.

Deciding that requests and petitions would not get them the kind of treatment they felt they needed, they resorted to direct actions varying from sitting in at welfare offices and destroying records and equipment to going into department stores and charging necessary goods to the welfare department. Although MAW did not gain all of its objectives, it did serve notice that welfare clients would no longer be passive, gratefully accepting whatever the society chose to give them.

Other welfare programs, usually dealing with surplus food, are conducted by the United States Department of Agriculture. Most of these programs serve both welfare and antipoverty purposes. The purchase of the surplus food from farmers is an antipoverty action. By purchasing crops from these farmers the government seeks to provide them with an adequate income from their occupation and thus prevent them from becoming poor. Critics charge that much of this "antipoverty money" goes to corporations or to large private farms which are clearly in no danger of slipping into poverty. The distribution of the surplus food by such means as food stamps is a welfare action. Cleosa Henley in "Lord, I'm Hungry" in Chapter 3 talks about the food stamp program. The sale of food stamps which allow poor people to obtain food at considerable savings is conducted through the cooperation of local county governments. As of 1968 millions of dollars appropriated for the food stamp program were turned back largely because many of the poorest counties, whether because of pride, discrimination, or fear of federal government interference, refused to participate in the program.

What Do You Think?

1. In 1968 New York City decided that the cost of investigating welfare claims was greater than the amount such investigations saved by keeping cheaters off the rolls. It dropped its program of investigation in favor of accepting the word of claimants. Should other cities do likewise?

2. Should the federal government set compulsory standards for welfare aid so that no recipients would have a reason to move from one state to another in search of better benefits?

3.   Do unemployable poor people have a right to adequate welfare benefits or should they be grateful for whatever the society gives them?

2.   ANTIPOVERTY PROGRAMS

What do antipoverty programs involve? Here are some examples:

America has had a tremendous antipoverty program going for over 300 years, although it wasn't usually thought of as such. The almost unbelievable growth of production in the United States provided a path out of poverty not only for millions of Americans but also for other millions who fled from poverty elsewhere in the world. Certainly, as noted in Chapter 2, not everyone shared equally in the fruits of this growth in production, but the average standard of living rose impressively and the percentage of the population that could be classed as living in poverty declined.

It was not until the Great Depression of the 1930's that the federal government became seriously concerned about developing programs to help those who had not shared in the plenty. The Depression shook confidence in the belief that the free economy would continue to expand until there was prosperity for all. The New Deal, at the same time that it sought to alleviate the sufferings of the unemployed, sought to establish governmental programs that would stimulate economic growth when private spending did not.

This problem was temporarily forced into the background as World War II provided jobs for the unemployed and others, particularly women, in defense industries.

In 1946 labor leaders and congressmen who were concerned that the end of the war would mean a return to Depression conditions attempted to push legislation through Congress that would commit the government to provide for full employment. No one, they argued, who wanted to work should be without a job. If private industry could not provide enough jobs, then the government should. The measure that was finally adopted as the Employment Act of 1946 was much weaker than they had desired and was concerned with maximum rather than full employment. It did, however, acknowledge the importance of maximum employment and recognize the government's responsibility to promote it.

In 1964 President Lyndon B. Johnson announced that the country was about to declare a "War on Poverty." Congress responded by passing the Economic Opportunity Act of 1964. Typical of the results of this act are the Job Corps and the establishment of Community Action Programs.

The idea behind the Job Corps is to bring to training centers young men and women who have dropped out of school and are either unemployed or employed in dead-end jobs. Some of these centers are located in the hearts of cities. In the centers the young people are encouraged to continue their general education, improve their physical condition, and, above all, learn useful skills. Some of the Job Corps centers have been praised as extremely effective; others have been condemned as ineffective at best and hangouts for juvenile delinquents at worst.

Under the Community Action Program provision, grants are given to public and private nonprofit groups to combat poverty in specific neighborhoods.

The Office of Economic Opportunity, which is in charge of these antipoverty programs, is also involved in helping people to help themselves through improving their health and mental health and, perhaps most controversially, by assisting those who wish help in planning the size of their families.

A number of business corporations are also involved in current antipoverty programs. The federal government frequently provides funds to assist in financing them or to pay the entire cost. Some private corporations have contracted to operate Job Corps centers. Others have adopted programs to train and provide employment for men and women previously considered unemployable.

The Raytheon Company, an electronics concern in suburban Boston, is a corporation with such a program. The undertaking began with 47 trainees in February, 1968. A bus chartered by the company brought these previously hard-core unemployed from the poor Roxbury section of the city to the suburbs each day. Instruction included both general educational courses, such as reading, and job training for positions which ranged from cable-making to drafting.

By July, 1968, the training of this first group had ended. At that time 35 of the trainees were working for the corporation and five were employed by other companies, were in the Job Corps, or had been drafted. Both company officials and community group leaders were enthusiastic about the program. They noted, for example, that only one of the 47 had been released from the program for poor behavior. This was far from what had been predicted by critics at the beginning of the program. Other companies, such as the Ford Motor Company and members of the Bell Telephone System, have reported similar results.

The main criticisms that have been leveled against these programs are that although they work well for those involved, they affect too few to have any real impact on poverty, and that they are too costly for either the taxpayer or the stockholder to bear.

There are also current programs operated entirely by the poor themselves. These include the formation of block or neighborhood action groups, which aim to improve living conditions, and the establishment of cooperatives and corporations, which will establish stores, manufacturing concerns, and banking, transportation, and other service units. These groups frequently encourage the affluent and leaders in the dominant communities to give support by purchasing stock or depositing money in the banks, but they insist on control by the poor.

Control by the poor themselves and community involvement have been unusually successful in some ventures and have brought problems in others.

Earlier readings have shown the extent of poverty in rural America and especially among farm workers. The major labor unions, including the A. F. of L.-C. I. O. and the Teamsters, have attempted to bring migrant workers together in unions to gain improvements, but by and large these efforts have not been very successful.

What Do You Think?

1. There are currently hundreds of different programs aimed at ending poverty in America. Some are run by the government, some by corporations, and some by groups of individuals. Should this variety be encouraged or should all efforts be combined into one massive nationwide program? Give your reasons.

2. Do private corporations have a responsibility to work for the elimination of poverty even if this means a reduction in the amount of dividends they can pay to their stockholders?

3. Which do you think holds most promise—welfare or anti-poverty programs? Explain.

3. CESAR CHAVEZ *

Another possibility is to organize the poor. The organization having most success in bringing the migrant grape pickers of California into a small, local union is one headed by former migrant worker Cesar Chavez. Here is a description of some of his efforts:

In Coachella, the pickets gather in the dark at three-thirty in the morning. By four o'clock they are on their way to the fields, their long

---

* Excerpted from Lincoln Richardson, "Cesar Chavez" in *Presbyterian Life,* October 1, 1968. Used by permission.

rows of headlights bouncing over the desert roads towards half-a-dozen different vineyards. By dawn they will be strung out along the sandy road-sides, in front of huge square patches of irrigated green in the sagebrush, and they will shout into the fields: *"Huelga!"*

Strike. Harvest and strike have come together in the far south of California. They will go on together through the summer heat, moving north together through the great chessboard grape valleys of California.

Already grapes, and enormous investments, are rotting. Even so, composure is the rule. Occasionally, it gives way to the frantic: a foreman in a pickup truck pinwheels off the road into a knot of pickets idling in the five o'clock heat, he scatters several who scramble to safety, and knocks two more painfully aside, then accelerates in the loose sand toward the field. Pickets swarm over the truck, pounding on the wind-shield, pulling open the doors, throwing sand into the cockpit, bringing it to a stop.

Sudden silence. The fierce foreman, quickly transformed, peers around from behind the wheel, blinking like a man who has lost his glasses; there is a trickle of blood across the bridge of his nose. The creator of silence is a short, erect man, who has just pulled the fiery captain of the pickets off the running board, and now looks easily around a circle of uneasy faces. The anger in the eyes of Cesar Chavez is well-contained in the steady gaze that has looked carefully at conflict and indignity, and is now confident, hopeful, and, always, calculating.

Addressing the ranking grower in the group, who has just driven in from San Francisco headquarters in a sports car, Chavez delivers a short purposeful speech. "This has got to stop. It's happening here. It's happening up north. The San Joaquin Valley is about to blow. We've got to have peace this summer. This has got to stop." In the face of a vigorous round of seconding speeches from the pickets, the grower also keeps his cool: "The foreman was wrong. *I said* he was wrong. What do you want me to do?"

Later, in the calm, the grower, who has shipping interests as well as land up and down the state, mentions that he has heard from an official in the longshoremens' union. The longshoremen have been supporting the pickers' strike; Cesar and the grower retire across the road for a talk. Cesar considers him a good guy with only one serious flaw: he won't sign a contract. "He says he would, but that he can't sign without the others. A lot of them say that."

Cesar climbs back into his car, beside the Reverend James Drake of the California Migrant Ministry, his administrative assistant and closest associate. They will make one more quick tour of the area. They have been cruising rapidly about since four o'clock; at almost six, work is underway. Striking a grape valley is a complex and difficult art, with no successful models. It is like striking a factory thirty miles across with thousands of entrances. Every row is an entrance. The chances of facing workers as they enter the fields are dim; pickets rely on loudspeakers, persuasive rhetoric and a show of numbers to persuade workers to come back out—"Join us, brothers. Leave the fields. Stand up for your rights."

Standing by the road in the early light, the pickets are mostly young, boys and girls who are already veterans at stoop labor. They have slept a short night on the floor, eaten donated food, and now seem exhilarated to be standing beside a field, and holding a red and black flag, ready to begin shouting into the field. Some are older, grayheaded men, who have also slept on the floor, and to whom austerity has already given dignity. Now, in austerity for a purpose, they have gained pride. Theirs is not the half-enchanted garrulity of the young, laced with laughter, but they too will shout: *"Huelga!"* Strike.

It is impossible to know exactly where the pickets should be, but it is Cesar's business, as director of the United Farm Workers' Organizing Committee, to know as much as possible, and he has learned to read the vineyard country well.

Few workers will leave the fields while the pickets are there. Many, however, do not return the next day. When the workers first come into the area—UFWOC openly suspects that many are recruited in Mexico and smuggled across the border—few of them have heard of the strike, or have even imagined a strike of farm workers. Striking has always seemed to be the exclusive privilege of industrial workers: when the Wagner Act in 1935 established the legal basis for workers to organize and bargain collectively, it excluded farm workers. Since then, most growers and workers alike have accepted that exclusion as natural. But now, Cesar Chavez is attempting to gain rights won by everyone else thirty years ago. He appears the more radical to his adversaries because of the very anachronism of his struggle. He is seen, not as a conservative who is thirty years late and trying to catch up, but rather as a radical, daring to challenge a tradition so very venerable.

*　　*　　*　　*　　*

[Later that day Cesar must leave for Delano, California. It was here that he began his organizing work in 1962. Cesar and his wife, Helen, have their home in Delano and the union office is located there.]

That evening, Cesar talks to five hundred cheerful, gently perspiring people packed into a hot hall on a hot night for a long program. It is a spirited, entertaining evening, with speeches interspersed, at just the right time, with songs, presentations (such as Scab of the Week, offered in absentia), and the important, skillful, satiric and historical dramatizations of the *Teatro de Campesinas*. (Since the early days of the strike, the *Teatro* has been an important means of expressing, clarifying, and dramatizing the issues at stake in the strike.) After the rally, Cesar and Helen go to dinner with a Teamster official. The competition between the slick, rich, traditional, and tough Teamsters and the new indigenous United Farm Workers had been a bitter struggle. Neither side has forgotten it, but each is able to see advantages in cooperation. Cesar and Helen arrive home at two o'clock, twenty-three hours after Cesar got up in Coachella.

Next morning, departure for Coachella is delayed by half-a-dozen pieces of business. There has been a personnel problem at the cooperative which, because the automobile is basic to the farm workers' economy, began as a gas station and parts shop. The co-op is run by the Reverend Fred Dresser, a successful grocer, who, after a late seminary education, joined the staff of the California Migrant Ministry. From the co-op, Cesar goes to the large new headquarters the union is building at the edge of town. The union had set up a large cross at the edge of the property; someone has set fire to it during the night. Then, after a second stop at the present office to pick up documents, they are off for Coachella.

The documents are contracts, and Drake reads the terms aloud as they drive south. Cesar does not negotiate contracts. "I can fight with them during a strike," he says, "but once they are beat, I haven't got the heart to negotiate."

What Do You Think?

1. Although still far from achieving all its goals, UFWOC has been more successful than earlier unions in organizing migrant farm workers. What accounts for this greater degree of success?

2. Is it proper for religious leaders and groups to become involved in activities such as those described in this selection?

4. THE CRUSADE FOR OPPORTUNITY

While Cesar Chavez's efforts have been much more successful than those of outside organizations in organizing the grape pickers, leadership by members of the local poverty community does not always guarantee success for programs. In some cases, it has seemed to lead to disaster for them. One such case can be found in the records of the Syracuse, New York, Crusade for Opportunity.

The Crusade developed as a Community Action Program receiving Office of Economic Opportunity funds. Various governmental, service, and religious groups worked together in the Crusade, conducting such programs as the Neighborhood Youth Corps and Head Start (designed to provide preschool training for disadvantaged youngsters to increase their chances for success in school).

O. E. O. guidelines for the operation of Community Action Programs in 1967 suggested that poor people constitute at least one-third of the representatives to the corporation running such a program. One-third was a minimum number, for the guidelines called for "maximum feasible participation" by the poor in the operation of the programs. In January, 1967, a group of militant representatives of the poor gained control of the corporation and voted enough new "poor" members in to assure themselves of continuing control. They declared that this was "maximum feasible participation."

Protests against actions taken by the Crusade under this new leadership were not long in coming. Many of the older service organizations ended their support. Members of the board of directors publicly opposed the new leadership and were suspended. Financial confusion and race and class hatred increased.

O. E. O. finally ended its financial support to the Crusade in October, 1967. Antipoverty programs in Syracuse were either cut back or eliminated entirely. Control by the poor had led to the downfall of the Crusade for Opportunity.

Why was this the result? Militants argued that when representatives who wanted real instead of token improvements for the poor took control, the establishment decided it had to kill the Crusade to protect itself. It accomplished this by hindering the Crusade from within and by working against it from the outside to get funds and support cut off. Opponents of the militants argued that those misleaders of the poor deliberately destroyed the Crusade to discredit the government and create a more revolutionary atmosphere. Less partial observers argued that it was not a case of evil intentions on either side but rather a problem of poor administration on the part of those who had been denied all previous opportunities to gain experience in that field and of poor communication on the part of middle-class people who had never learned to talk with the poor.[3]

A similar crisis arose in New York City in the fall of 1968 over the actions of the governing board chosen by residents of the poor Ocean Hill-Brownsville District of Brooklyn to run the schools in their area. The objective in creating this small school district within the huge New York City District was to see if community control would lead to better education and thus help disadvantaged children to break out of the slums. The conflict between the governing board and "the establishment,"

---

[3] A more detailed discussion of this crisis can be found in Lawrence Davis, "Syracuse: What Happens When the Poor Take Over," in *The Reporter,* March 21, 1968.

in this case the teachers' union, led to strikes and a dangerous increase in racial tension.

The same interpretations of the trouble were given as were heard in Syracuse: the result of the establishment's attempting to keep the poor down but quiet; the result of militant attempts to promote riot and revolution; and of well-intended mistakes by inexperienced people.

What Do You Think?

1.   Are there really individuals or groups who want to see the failure of antipoverty programs? If so, who and why? If not, why are such charges made?

2.   Who knows best what actions are needed to improve the conditions of the poor: government officials, professors, successful businessmen, or poor people themselves?

5.   POOR PEOPLE MARCH ON GOVERNMENT

Next is an example of the poor taking action themselves. Would you endorse this kind of activity?

During the summer of 1968 poor people from all over the United States marched on Washington, D. C., to call upon the federal government to take effective action to improve their lot. Dr. Martin Luther King, Jr., had begun the planning for the march before his assassination.

While in Washington the poor built a "Resurrection City," testified before governmental agencies and congressional committees, demonstrated, and committed some acts of civil disobedience. They also presented several lists of demands. One list, issued by Bayard Rustin, included a call for an "economic bill of rights" that would grant certain guarantees:

Every employable citizen has the right to a meaningful job at decent wages. The poor are not lazy. In fact the vast majority toil long hours at menial, underpaid labor. Their wages must be raised. New careers must be created for them—in building decent housing for all; in raising the level of education, health and social care; in reconstructing and beautifying America. This is not makework. This is meaningful work that goes to the heart of our nation's needs.

Every citizen who cannot work be guaranteed an adequate income as a matter of right. A thousand economists of varying persuasions have called for a guaranteed annual income as morally necessary and economically sound.[4]

The Rustin list also included such specific demands as:

1. Institute food distribution programs wherever severe hunger exists in America.
2. Provide free food stamps to those who cannot afford to buy them.
3. Help poor farmers set up cooperatives.
4. Give the poor first priority in existing health programs and create health services in isolated rural areas.
5. Include the poor in the planning and administration of Federal programs at local levels.[5]

The poor marchers had few immediate gains to show for their efforts. One magazine reported on the attitude in Washington toward the marchers saying:

> Before Resurrection City was closed last week, some dim-witted park policemen were firing tear gas canisters into the camp wholesale (85 rounds), apparently in order to stop rowdies from throwing rocks at cars. The action reflected the mood in the city and in the federal government. To hell with the poor. Everyone is sick of them. They are dirty, immoral, surly, and unreasonable. They have ruined the image we wish to have of them as proper little beggars.[6]

There was a reaction against the behavior of the poor in confronting the government right in Washington. There was also a feeling that, although it would be nice to end poverty, the country just could not afford it while in the midst of a war in Vietnam. Other voices were heard, however, saying that it could be done if the government and the nation were willing to face up to the real issues involved.

What Do You Think?

1. Was the Poor People's March a success or a failure? Explain.
2. Rustin says "the poor are not lazy." Would you agree? Why or why not?
3. Should every citizen who cannot work be guaranteed an adequate income as a matter of right? Why or why not?

---

[4] Excerpted from *The New York Times,* June 3, 1968.
[5] Excerpted from *The New York Times,* June 3, 1968.
[6] Excerpted from "Get Out of Town," *The New Republic,* July 6, 1968.

6.   FINANCING A POVERTY PROGRAM *

Business Week, *a magazine for executives, examined the country's economic situation and then outlined the steps the nation could take if it really wanted to do something to assist the poor without endangering the economy. It spoke out in an editorial appearing while the poverty marchers were still in Washington.*

Just a few years ago Michael Harrington wrote a book about "The Other America"—that is, about poor Americans, who he said were "invisible" in this rich country. The poor are still with us but they are no longer invisible; indeed, the Poor People's March on Washington is only dramatizing what has already become the most conspicuous—and difficult—issue in American politics.

The issue is the most difficult because of the deep resistances to paying the heavy costs of bridging the gap between the many who are affluent and the far too many who live wretchedly in this country. Unless the issue is posed in that way, there is the temptation to talk a lot of pious cant about the problems of the poor.

The simple arithmetic is this: To raise the present incomes of 30-million Americans up to the poverty line of $3,000 per year for a family of four persons would cost a minimum of $11-billion. However, economists who have worked in this area consider that figure far too low for a program with any hope of really moving people out of poverty; they calculate that the annual cost of a barely adequate program would be at least $20-billion above present federal anti-poverty spending.

But such numbers are being proposed at a time when the federal budget is already in heavy deficit. The immediate fight between the White House and Congressional conservatives is over whether to cut federal expenditures by either $4-billion or $6-billion, while increasing taxes by more than $10-billion in order to reduce the fiscal 1969 budget deficit to only $8-billion or so.

Does this mean that the situation is really hopeless, and that politicians and businessmen who are simultaneously decrying poverty and preaching fiscal restraint are talking out of both sides of their mouths? In part, it does. But, more fundamentally, it means that practically no one has faced up to the hard issue of reconciling a redistribution of income toward the poor with fiscal prudence.

Fiscal restraint is required to keep this country from falling into a

---

national and international financial catastrophe. Inflation may not seem to disturb the nation overly much while the boom is on. But when the boom busts, the pains become universally palpable. If the U. S. should elect to persist on an inflationary course, paying for all sorts of government programs by depreciating the currency, it will increasingly be driven to protectionism, governmental controls and manipulation of foreign exchange, and finally economic isolation, which will have grave political as well as economic costs.

But pointing out these fundamental dangers does not mean that the country should not tackle the crucial problems of domestic poverty. Nor does it mean that much larger resources cannot go to the poor without damaging the national economy.

THE THREE FUNDAMENTALS

How can this trick be worked? There is no magic, but it will involve sticking to three principles:

1. The present composition of government expenditures must be restructured to focus more resources on the people at the bottom of society. There is merit in the complaint of Mrs. Martin Luther King that "our Congress passes laws which subsidize corporation farms, oil companies, airlines, and houses for suburbia, but when it turns its attention to the poor it suddenly becomes concerned about balancing the budget." In this time of inflation, the nation does need to worry—and should worry more—about balancing the budget, but there is no reason in the world (other than pork-barrel politics) that costly programs subsidizing individuals or groups that are quite well fixed should not be cut down or out, and replaced by subsidies for those who really need help.

2. Existing programs for helping the poor need to be improved or replaced. According to government estimates, some $27-billion of federal money is already going to the poor—plus a lot of state and local money. Many of these programs, in the opinion of welfare experts, suffer from deficiencies that lock the poor into poverty—for instance, by making it impossible for a husband to stay with his family or next to impossible for a woman to get day care for her children and go out to work. Welfare's faults have been studied and restudied; we know what to do. The need is to replace study with action.

3. A growing economy can afford, and will benefit from, programs to lift people out of poverty. The so-called "fiscal dividend"— the increasing tax yield of a growing economy—will total $10-billion or more every year. We should devote a larger share of these increasing resources to creating the jobs, providing services

such as education and health that will prepare people for employment, and, when necessary, maintaining the income of those who cannot work or cannot support their families with the low-paying jobs for which they can qualify.

None of this will come easily. It will involve hard thought and careful planning of where government spending is going. If we are serious about licking the poverty problem in this country, we should put our money—and our private and public planning—where until now only our mouths have been.

What Do You Think?

1. The three principles outlined in the editorial are not really new. Why haven't they been put into practice?

2. The editorial speaks of financial problems and pressures existing at the time of the Poor People's March and the way in which they made it difficult to eliminate poverty without harming the nation's economy. Do such problems and pressures still exist today? Will it become easier or more difficult to afford to end poverty in the future?

7. ECONOMIC PROPOSALS FOR THE ALLEVIATION OF POVERTY

Two of the provisions of the "economic bill of rights," full employment and a guaranteed annual income, have received considerable attention as the ways in which the nation's money and planning could be put where its mouth has been.

The Main Attack Upon Poverty: Economic Performance

Plans to attack poverty through increased employment, employment in jobs which actually contribute to American production rather than "makework" jobs, are based on the assumption that the poor need dignity as well as money and that useful work contributes to dignity.

The key to ending poverty, according to one group of experts, is increased employment achieved by more rapid economic growth:

Let us now sum up our conclusions about the roots and offshoots of poverty. While many living in poverty have lost ambition and hope, the programs which would draw them into the march of progress would restore ambition and hope. While we need enlarged education and training, we should reject the slogan that "I never knew an educated man who was poor"; most college-trained people acquired this advantage because their parents were not poor, and many senior citizens with college degrees are poor. The contrast between unemployment of only 670 thousand in 1944, and more than 4 million now, does not mean that six times as many people are unfitted for work because of changing job qualifications; predominantly, it means fewer job openings relative to the number of people needing jobs. Drawing a hundred thousand or more young people a year into youth programs, where they will receive opportunities to work and to learn, is all to the good; but about *16 million* children cannot be rescued from their current poverty if their parents are neglected, and their parents can be rescued only in the context of our performing economic system. And while millions of the poor, due to old age or disabilities, cannot in the main be accorded jobs at good pay, the improved performance of the whole economic system would yield more public revenues from which to allocate more income and services to them; conversely, their enlarged purchasing power would help the whole economic system. All this indicates that sustained maximum employment, production, and purchasing power under the Employment Act of 1946—properly conceived—would provide the main key to all these problems.[7]

Proposals for a Guaranteed Annual Income

Another series of proposals for the alleviation of poverty is based on the idea that money is the key; that if the poor are given an adequate income they will be able to meet their own needs and overcome the ill effects of poverty by themselves. These are the proposals for a guaranteed annual income similar to the one included in Rustin's "economic bill of rights."

The type of guaranteed income that is most frequently discussed is a "negative income tax." Many variations have been proposed. In 1968 the federal government entered into a contract which called for trying out several different types in New Jersey on a limited scale for the purpose of determining which was most effective.

Most proposed negative income taxes are built around an estimate of the amount of money needed per year by a family if it is to escape from poverty conditions. The amounts are usually around $3,000 to $3,300.

The most costly proposal calls for the federal government to give each family the difference between the amount it earns and the escape from poverty figure. Thus if the government decides that if a family of

---

[7] Excerpted from Leon H. Keyserling, *Progress or Poverty: The U. S. at the Crossroads.* Washington, D. C.: Conference on Economic Progress, 1964.

four needs $3,000 to avoid poverty and members of that family earn only $1,600, the federal government would pay that family a negative income tax of $1,400. This would replace existing welfare programs. Critics charge that this would destroy initiative since each family would be guaranteed an adequate income whether anyone worked or not. A modified program calls for the federal government to give half of the difference between the amount earned and the amount needed to avoid poverty. Its supporters maintain that this would cost less and would be less likely to encourage idleness. Critics who want to see a more generous program point out that it would not, however, end poverty.

Another variation on the negative income tax would allow poor families to profit as affluent families do from having dependents. An affluent taxpayer with a wife and three children, for example, can deduct $600 each for five people (self, wife, and children), or a total of $3,000 from his income, before figuring his taxes, and thus reduce the amount he has to pay the government. Under a negative income tax of this type the poor individual with the same number of dependents would be given as much by the government as his affluent friend saves in taxes. Critics say that while this would not have the same ill effect of breaking up families that ADC now has, it is still too similar to that current program. They also fear that it might encourage the poor to have more children and thus receive more from the government.

Each plan that has been proposed has had its critics. Yet many experts still believe that this nation could find a way to eliminate poverty. Because they see it as unnecessary in this affluent society, they see it as a national disgrace. There are others who disagree, saying that it is not a national problem but one which the poor must solve for themselves. And the debate goes on.

Is poverty in America a personal problem, or is it a national disgrace?

What Do You Think?

1. It costs much more to teach a person a new skill than it does to provide food, clothing, and shelter for him through welfare. Is it worth the extra cost? Explain.

2. Representatives of the poor have demanded an economic bill of rights. Do Americans have as much of a right to the economic conditions listed on pages 100–101 as they do to the political freedoms in the existing Bill of Rights?

3. Which of the programs listed here, either current or proposed, would go farthest toward eliminating poverty from America? Defend your choice.

ACTIVITIES FOR INVOLVEMENT

1.   Have members of the class visit as many welfare and antipoverty offices (Welfare, Urban Renewal, Office of Economic Opportunity, Job Corps, Community Action Program, etc.) as possible and interview officials. The interviews should seek information about the nature of the program, how successful it is, and the reasons for its success or failure. The interviews should be reported to the class as the basis for a discussion of the scope, effectiveness, and problems of current programs.

2.   If it is not possible to conduct the interviews outlined in Question 1, have groups in the class do research into each of the programs to uncover the information needed for the discussion.

3.   The poor people's march that took place during May and June 1968 did not achieve its objectives. Make a study of the march to discover the reasons for this failure. Report the results of your study.

4.   Have a committee consider the various alternative proposals for a negative income tax and draft a proposed bill calling for the adoption of the version they think best. Conduct a mock congressional debate on the merits of the bill in class.

5.   Write an essay answering the question, "Is poverty a personal problem or a national disgrace?"

BIBLIOGRAPHY
For Further Study

BIBLIOGRAPHY
For Further Study

Books

EVERETT, ROBINSON O. (ed.) · *Anti-Poverty Programs* · Dobbs Ferry, N. Y.: Oceana Publications, 1966.

FERMAN, LOUIS A., KORNBLUH, JOYCE L., and HABER, ALAN (eds.) · *Poverty in America: A Book of Readings* · Ann Arbor, Mich.: Univ. of Michigan Press, 1965.

GALBRAITH, JOHN KENNETH · *The Affluent Society* · Boston, Mass.: Houghton Mifflin Company, 1958.

GANS, HERBERT J. · *The Urban Villagers: Group and Class in the Life of Italian Americans* · New York, N. Y.: Free Press of Glencoe, Inc., 1962.

GLAZER, NATHAN, and MOYNIHAN, DANIEL PATRICK · *Beyond the Melting Pot* · Cambridge, Mass.: Massachusetts Institute of Technology Press, 1963.

LEWIS, OSCAR · *La Vida: A Puerto Rican Family in the Culture of Poverty— San Juan and New York* · New York, N. Y.: Random House, 1966.

MAY, EDGAR · *The Wasted Americans: Cost of Our Welfare Dilemma* · New York, N. Y.: Harper & Row, 1964.

MYRDAL, GUNNAR · *Challenge to Affluence* · New York, N. Y.: Random House, 1963.

RIIS, JACOB A. · *How the Other Half Lives: Studies Among the Tenements of New York* · New York, N. Y.: Charles Scribner's Sons, 1918.

SHOTWELL, LOUISA R. · *The Harvesters: The Story of the Migrant People* · Garden City, N. Y.: Doubleday & Company, Inc., 1961.

SIMON, ARTHUR · *Faces of Poverty* · St. Louis, Mo.: Concordia Publishing House, 1966.

WATTENBERG, BEN J. and SCAMMON, RICHARD M. · *This U. S. A.: An Unexpected Family Portrait of 194,067,296 Americans Drawn from the Census* · Garden City, N. Y.: Doubleday & Company, Inc., 1966.

WELLER, JACK E. · *Yesterday's People—Life in Contemporary Appalachia* · Louisville, Ky.: Univ. of Kentucky Press, 1965.

WILSON, JAMES Q. (ed.) · *The Metropolitan Enigma: Inquiries into the Nature and Dimensions of America's "Urban Crisis"* · Washington, D. C.: Chamber of Commerce of the United States, 1967.

WOYTINSKY, EMMA S. · *Profile of the U. S. Economy: A Survey of Growth and Change* · New York, N. Y.: Frederick A. Praeger, 1967.

Reports

COLEMAN, JAMES S. *et al* · *Equality of Educational Opportunity* · Washington, D. C.: U. S. Government Printing Office, 1966.

FORD, THOMAS R., (ed.) · *The Southern Appalachian Region: A Survey* · Lexington, Ky.: Univ. of Kentucky Press, 1962.

Hungry Children · Special Report of the Southern Regional Council, Atlanta, Ga., 1967.

The People Left Behind, A Report by the President's National Advisory Commission on Rural Poverty · Washington, D. C.: U. S. Government Printing Office, 1967.

Report of the National Advisory Commission on Civil Disorders · Washington, D. C.: U. S. Government Printing Office, 1968.

Paperback Books

BALDWIN, JAMES · *The Fire Next Time* · New York, N. Y.: Dell Publishing Company, 1962.

BROWN, CLAUDE · *Manchild in the Promised Land* · New York, N. Y.: New American Library, 1965.

CAUDILL, HARRY · *Night Comes to the Cumberlands* · Boston, Mass.: Little, Brown & Co., 1963.

CONANT, JAMES B. · *Slums and Suburbs* · New York, N. Y.: McGraw-Hill, 1961.

CONOT, ROBERT · *Rivers of Blood, Years of Darkness* · New York, N. Y.: Bantam Books, 1967.

FISHMAN, LEO, (ed.) · *Poverty Amid Affluence* · New Haven, Conn.: Yale Univ. Press, 1966.

GAVIN, JAMES M., with HADLEY, ARTHUR T. · *Crisis Now* · New York, N. Y.: Random House, 1968.

HARRINGTON, MICHAEL · *The Other America: Poverty in the United States* · Baltimore, Md.: Penguin Books, 1963.

HUNTER, DAVID R. · *The Slums, Challenge and Response, 2nd ed.* · New York, N. Y.: Free Press of Glencoe, 1968.

JACOBS, PAUL *et al* · *Dialogue on Poverty* · New York, N. Y.: Bobbs-Merrill Company, Inc., 1967.

KAUFMAN, BEL · *Up the Down Staircase* · Englewood Cliffs, N. J.: Prentice-Hall, Inc., 1964.

KEYSERLING, LEON H. · *Progress or Poverty: The U. S. at the Crossroads* · Washington, D. C.: Conference on Economic Progress, 1964.

KOZOL, JONATHAN · *Death at an Early Age* · Boston, Mass.: Houghton Mifflin Company, 1967.

POTTER, DAVID M. · *People of Plenty: Economic Abundance and the American Character* · Chicago, Ill.: The Univ. of Chicago Press, 1954.

SHOSTAK, ARTHUR B., and GOMBERG, WILLIAM, (eds.) · *New Perspectives on Poverty* · Englewood Cliffs, N. J.: Prentice-Hall, Inc., 1965.

THOMAS, PIRI · *Down These Mean Streets* · New York, N. Y.: The New American Library, 1967.

Articles

ALSOP, JOSEPH · "No More Nonsense About Ghetto Education," *New Republic,* Vol. 157, July 22, 1967.

BAGDIKIAN, BEN H. · "Black Immigrants," *The Saturday Evening Post,* Vol. 240, July 15, 1967.

BATTLE, MARK · "Speaking Out; Whitey Can't Help the Black Ghetto," *The Saturday Evening Post,* Vol. 239, January 29, 1966.

CARMICHAEL, STOKLEY, *et al* · "Black Ghettoes," (A Special Section), *Atlantic Monthly,* Vol. 220, October, 1967.

"Invisible Poor of the Garden State," *Commonweal,* Vol. 86, Sept. 8, 1967.

"Is U. S. Really Filled With Poverty?—A Reply," *New Republic,* Vol. 157, October 7, 1967.

HARRIS, LADONNA (Mrs. Fred) · "Warpaint for the Senator's Wife," *Look,* Vol. 31, April 4, 1967.

JACOBS, PAUL · "How It Is, Getting on Welfare," *Harper's Magazine,* Vol. 235, October, 1967.

LAMALE, HELEN H. · "Poverty: The Word and the Reality," *Monthly Review,* July, 1965.

"Mississippi: Starving By the Rule Book," *The Nation,* Vol. 204, April 3, 1967.

OSHIN, E. S. · "Here Today But Where Tomorrow?" *The New York Times Magazine,* March 5, 1967.

"Permanent Insurrection," *National Review,* Vol. 19, August 8, 1967.

ROWAN, H. · "The Minority Nobody Knows," (Mexican-Americans), *Atlantic Monthly,* Vol. 219, June, 1967.

SHERRILL, R. · "It Isn't True That Nobody Starves in America," *The New York Times Magazine,* June 4, 1967.

"Should the Federal Government Guarantee a Minimum Annual Income to All Citizens?" *Congressional Digest,* Vol. 46, October, 1966.

SPENCER, DAVID · "A Harlem Parent Speaks," *NEA Journal,* Vol. 57, March, 1968.

"The Unjolly Green Giant," *Commonweal,* Vol. 86, July 28, 1967.

"Vietnam and the Poor," (an editorial), *The Saturday Evening Post,* Vol. 240, February 25, 1967.

Films and Tapes

At Home, 2001 (30 min; color; Modern Talking Picture Service Inc.) · A part of the *21st Century* series. Shows the direction in which the affluent mainstream of America is moving and provides a good contrast when shown with materials on the poor.

The Battle of Newburgh (54 min; B/W; McGraw-Hill; 2 reels) · An award winning NBC 1963 "White Paper" presentation examining the struggle over the efforts by City Manager Joseph Mitchell to cut welfare costs in the New York town. Interviews with people on welfare.

Cities and the Poor (120 min. in two parts of 60 min. each; B/W; NET-Indiana Univ.) · Part I examines the conditions, problems, and frustrations of the poor in Chicago and Los Angeles. Part II examines unrest and explores current antipoverty programs and their weaknesses.

Edge of Abundance (60 min; B/W; NET-Indiana Univ.) · An examination of the automated and technologically advanced American economy and the impact that such advances have on employment, education, and values.

Exploding the Myths of Prejudice (color; Human Relations Series; Warren Schloat Productions, Inc.) · Discusses the myths and misconceptions underlying racial prejudice, pointing out that prejudices are the learned results of an individual's social environment.

Good Night, Socrates (34 min; B/W; Contemporary Films, N. Y. and San Francisco) · A small boy in an American city watches the destruction of his poor Greek neighborhood to make way for urban renewal. A sensitive film which challenges the idea that the thing to do about poverty is to put everybody into the same middle-class American mold.

Growing Up Black (color; Human Relations Series; Warren Schloat Productions, Inc.) · Reveals the realities of black childhood in our society.

Harvest of Shame (54 min; B/W; McGraw-Hill) · A "CBS Reports" investigation of the conditions under which migrant farm laborers live and the attitudes of more affluent people toward them. Extremely effective.

The Last Citizen (Tape series; 30 min ea; Univ. of Colorado, National Tape Repository) · The condition and treatment of the Negro. Of special value are the three tapes, "The City—A Place to Live," "The Last School House," and "The Last Migrant."

Marked for Failure (60 min; B/W; NET-Indiana Univ.) · The problems of the slum schools. Why these schools fail and, as a result, why slum children are not likely to enter the economic mainstream of America.

Minorities Have Made America Great (Parts 1 and 2) (color; Human Relations Series; Warren Schloat Productions, Inc.) · Each filmstrip reveals the many problems faced by a particular minority group and recounts its contributions to American life. Part 1 includes Negroes, Jews, Germans, and Irish; Part 2 includes American Indians, Orientals, Puerto Ricans, and Mexican-Americans.

My Own Yard To Play In (7 min; B/W; Contemporary Films, Inc., N. Y. and San Francisco) · An art film showing children of varying ethnic groups displaying imagination and joy as they play in a slum environment. Challenges the idea that the poor are "they," a group born different and inferior.

Neighborhood Story (30 min; B/W; Syracuse Univ.) · The role of the settlement house in the slum area.

Nothing But A Man (92 min; B/W; Brandon Films, Inc., N. Y., Chicago, and San Francisco) · A feature movie about the struggle of a sensitive, working class Negro in the South to achieve and maintain a sense of his own identity and manhood. Engrossing and effective.

Old Age—The Wasted Years (60 min; B/W; NET-Indiana Univ.) · The limited opportunities and living arrangements available to older people.

Rush Toward Freedom (color; Human Relations Series; Warren Schloat Productions, Inc.) · Five filmstrips show dramatic social revolution of the civil rights movement. Discusses violence, confrontation, direct action.

Shop Town (6 min; B/W; Brandon Films, Inc., N. Y., Chicago, and San Francisco) · A brief film showing the effects of technological unemployment.

Superfluous People (54 min; B/W; McGraw-Hill) · Welfare aid is seen as both a material and a moral problem. The film looks at people in trouble.

They Have Overcome (color; Human Relations Series; Warren Schloat Productions, Inc.) · Award-winning filmstrips documenting the achievements of five prominent Negroes in the face of enormous odds (Gordon Parks, Claude Brown, Dr. James Comer, Dr. Dorothy Brown, Charles Lloyd).

They Follow the Seasons (Tape; 13 min; Univ. of Colorado, National Tape Repository) · A church-produced tape on the lot of the migrant worker.

Three Cures for a Sick City (30 min; B/W; NET-Indiana Univ.) · An examination of different methods of urban renewal with the advantages and problems of each. The three examples are taken from Washington, D. C.

Threescore and Five (Tape Series; 30 min ea; Univ. of Colorado, National Tape Repository) · A series of tapes on the problems of aging. Of special interest are three: "In Sickness and in Health," "Income—The Greatest Need," and "Roof Over My Head."

Troubled Cities (60 min; B/W; NET-Indiana Univ.) · Attempts by New York, Detroit, Boston, and Newark to meet such critical urban problems as poor housing, racial unrest, and crime.